# A DECADE OF CHANGE

# A DECADE OF CHANGE

**Mark Darby, Paul Higgins, Neil Higson and Adrian Kenny**

Ian Allan
PUBLISHING

### Front cover

The magnificent Scottish scenery is set almost to perfection in this view of Nos 37417 *Richard Trevithick* and 37401 *The Royal Scotsman* skirting the side of Loch Carron with a Northern Belle trip, the 1Z37 08.53 Aberdeen-Kyle of Lochalsh on Sunday 7 August 2005.

The Northern Belle train was formed by parent company Venice-Simplon Orient Express in 2000 as an equally luxurious sister train to its more well known brown and cream liveried set of Pullman carriages. The train is certainly well-travelled, visiting destinations ranging from Inverness and Oban to Plymouth and London. *Adrian Kenny*

### Title Page

Class 37s Nos 37605 and 37611 hammer through the beautiful rural surroundings near Easenhall, Warwickshire on the Trent Valley line, as they haul the 4Z44 the 06.28 Coatbridge-Daventry DIRFT on the final few miles of their long journey. This Direct Rail Services (DRS)-run intermodal service linking Northamptonshire's Daventry International Rail Freight Terminal to Scotland was operated on behalf of the Malcolm Group with this particular service carrying goods for supermarket giant Asda.

Since the photograph was taken on 17 October 2003, DRS has increased its Anglo-Scottish intermodal traffic significantly with the latest high-profile operation being the 'Tesco Express' that has seen No 66411 painted in the colours of Eddie Stobart, a partner in this highly successful operation. A massive extension to the terminal (DIRFT 2) is planned and will feature a new rail hub. Planning consent has been obtained to build 1.945 million sq ft of new terminal which will see a big increase in rail service to this inland port. *Paul Higgins*

First Published 2008

ISBN 978 0 7110 3310 8

© Mark Darby, Paul Higgins, Neil Higson and Adrian Kenny

Published by Ian Allan Publishing Ltd, Hersham, Surrey KT12 4RG
Printed by Ian Allan Printing Ltd, Hersham Surrey KT12 4RG.

Code: 0809/B3

Visit the Ian Allan Publishing website at www.ianallanpublishing.com

# Introduction

This collection of images does not set out to be a definitive account of locomotive and multiple-unit classes, rolling stock or train consists. Neither does it attempt to visit every main corridor or byway branch line up and down the land. It is a portrayal of the former BR system during this first decade of privatisation – a period that has seen immense changes to the operation of the network and the trains that run on it. We have tried to cover the country as best we can, to illustrate some of the many liveries and workings observed over the last decade or so. It has been a 'Decade of Change' that has seen a mass exodus from the rather drab former British Rail blue & grey era, through the application of a small but not insignificant selection of Sectorisation 'paint jobs' and brandings and then on into the colourful world of private operators, who have projected their own eye-catching house colours and brandings on to the rail network. In the face of dwindling motive power variety, livery combinations began to create an interest in their own right.

Our aim for this album is to capture as many diverse company mixtures and corporate colour schemes passing through attractive countryside locations, or against the backdrop of some of the interesting older infrastructure that has managed to escape the onslaught of modern day progress. We have concentrated mainly, but not exclusively, on the locomotive-hauled passenger and freight scene as the variety of unit liveries would merit a book all of its own. The captions and preface are accurate to the end of 2007.

In preparing the book, we considered presenting the pictures in geographical order, class order, author order, alphabetical livery order and date order, but felt that, for one reason or another, none of these worked particularly well. Therefore we have decided upon a 'random' approach, so that the reader will constantly be kept guessing as to what will appear next and, hopefully at least, be pleasantly surprised by the picture he or she does see.

### Locomotive-hauled passenger trains

Locomotive-hauled passenger trains have been steadily declining since the introduction of the hugely successful and reliable High Speed Train (HST) on the Western Region back in 1976. Thirty-one years later, locomotive-hauled coaching stock is almost a thing of the past, but 'out west', the HST still reigns supreme.

The only parts of the country to benefit from regular timetabled locomotive-hauled services are London Liverpool Street to Ipswich and Norwich using ex-Virgin Class 90s; and the East Coast main line from London Kings Cross to Leeds and Scotland, with its former GNER Class 91-powered

*No 92024 JS Bach passes through Sevington, Kent with 4M44, the 18.10 Dollands Moor to Wembley service, bang on time on Sunday 23 July 2006. This EWS intermodal train carries containers from various parts of Europe to destinations across the UK.*

*The Class 92s were built between 1993 and 1996 by Brush Traction at Loughborough and can run at either 750V dc, as at Sevington, or under the wires at 25kV ac. The 46 locomotives built have never been fully utilised, even though they cost over £3 million each! The 6760hp (ac) 5360hp (dc) machines spend many hours stabled in yards, or in the case of the seven Eurostar machines, in store at Crewe.*

*Sadly one of the major problems has been the lack of growth in the Channel Tunnel traffic. The traffic levels predicted in 1995 have, in reality, never materialised. Neil Higson*

expresses. Hired-in Class 67 and 90 locomotives power the London to Scotland overnight sleeper services for ScotRail and First Great Western's small stud of four Class 57/6s work the nightly 'beds' to Cornwall.

As with all rules, there are exceptions though, with 'engine and coaches', appearing up and down the land working on behalf of the ever-popular charter market, using spot hire and heritage traction. There are also seasonal workings to various holiday resorts and diverted traffic that require haulage of electrically powered vehicles over non-electrified routes, along with the occasional rescue of recalcitrant trains.

In 2006, Dellner coupler-fitted Virgin 57/3s could still be seen hauling Pendolino sets between Crewe and Holyhead along the picturesque North Wales coast line. Unfortunately, these trains, at the time of writing, are expected to finish in December 2008.

The recent past has witnessed several locomotive-hauled services slip into oblivion, notably along the Midlands corridor from Euston, which saw a brief reprieve with the re-introduction of Driving Van Trailer (DVT) sets on the Northampton 'Cobbler' commuter trains. However, these only lasted a short time and ceased in July 2005. The move towards Pendolino units has been responsible for the almost complete eradication of the Class 86s and 87s. Freightliner still has an allocation of '86s' on its books, which, aside from Network Rail's few examples, form the only remaining 'AL6s' on the network, as Anglia's attractive turquoise-liveried examples have now been retired from service. The 1973-1975 British Rail Engineering Ltd-built Class 87s are, since the end of 2007, but a memory, with the former Virgin, GBRf, Fragonset and Cotswold examples all now withdrawn. There is, however, if one fancies a trip to Eastern Europe, the chance to photograph two of the former celebrity examples; Network SouthEast liveried, '2012 Olympic Bid'-branded No 87012 and former LNWR black-liveried No 87019, which

Porterbrook has leased to a Bulgarian freight operator, with the possibility of more to follow.

North of the border, EWS Class 90s coupled to a short rake of redundant ex-Virgin Mk 3s and a DVT performed shuttle service on the line to North Berwick, a service which ceased at the end of the summer 2005 timetable.

In the principality of Wales, we have witnessed the passing into history of the much lamented, mainly 'Syphon' (Class 37)-hauled, Cardiff Central to Rhymney commuter services. 'The Rhymneys' as they were known countrywide amongst the enthusiast fraternity, proved extremely popular with both punters and photographers alike. With such a limited selection of interesting trains to photograph, some locations could resemble a bit of a free-for-all, therefore alternative viewpoints became much sought after luxuries.

Also in Wales were the summer-dated runs to Fishguard Harbour, which used resources from the Rhymney trips. Although expensive to run and with awkward crewing arrangements, the trains were nevertheless well patronised and often full to the point of standing.

The traditional railway engine base colour of black is definitely used to good effect when the yellow logos of the Mediterranean Shipping Company are added to the bodyside. No 66709 *Joseph Arnold Davis* (the name coming from the company's Managing Director's father), is one of the second batch of Class 66/7s to be put to work by GBRf, which is now a subsidiary of FirstGroup plc.

It seems that never a month goes by without this company announcing a new rail haulage contract, with intermodal, engineering and now coal services being the main focus. The train depicted is a typical GBRf working, taken on 24 October 2006. A completely full 4L22 14.10 Hams Hall to Felixstowe train approaches Long Buckby village on the Northampton loop line. These trains operate twice a day on behalf of Medite and rarely have any empty space. *Paul Higgins*

For four days in July, the Royal Welsh Show at Builth Wells proved such a popular draw that an additional train was run especially for the event, which brought locomotive hauled services back to the Heart of Wales line. Unfortunately, in 2007, the number of units available was sufficient that there was no need for the locomotive-hauled trains for the first time in nine years. Gone now, seemingly forever, are the days of timetabled '37s' or '50s' providing a fine visual and audible spectacle in the far flung depths of Wales.

## Locomotive-hauled freight traffic

Here lies a rich seam of fascinating workings to be explored in terms of commodities, sources, destinations, wagon types and colour schemes. Freight trains are in many ways harder to photograph than their passenger brethren, seemingly suffering from cancellations, early running, late running, re-routing and other changes far more often than their passenger type counterpart. But the challenge of getting that unique shot on a branch line which can see as little as one train a week is rewarding, providing that the camera has worked, the setting is right and the focusing correct! This applies especially to Wales and Scotland where the weather often plays a more critical role in the taking of a shot.

There are literally hundreds of commodities carried by freight trains and the few paragraphs that we have available here cannot even attempt to do this enticing area justice. Suffice to say, coal, steel, petroleum, aggregate and container traffic form the majority of the bulk cargoes on the system today. Even within those categories, if one were to explore a bit more deeply, there lies a captivating variety of products. Coal can be in the form of a steam coal for the power generation market, anthracite for household use, or coking coal for the industrial sector.

Steel comes in many forms – slab, hot rolled coil, cold reduced coil, flat plate, tin or zinc coated, galvanised, colour coated, and so on. Aluminium, scrap and wire products also play a small but significant part in the railfreight metals scene. Each product is suited to a particular application and rail hauls everything from the raw materials to make it in the first place, through to the semi-finished and finished products, all over the country.

Petroleum ranges in substance from the 'heavy' boiler fuel end of the spectrum to the 'lighter' fractions, such as petrol, diesel and gas oil, all of which are carried by rail.

Aggregates are an ever fluctuating market. The likes of Mendip Rail haul literally millions of tonnes of year from HeidelbergCement AG's (formerly Hanson) and Holcim's (formerly Foster Yeoman) respective quarries in the Mendips to all sorts of destinations in the southeast of the country. The other main quarrying areas of the Peak Forest and Leicestershire see EWS and Freightliner providing services for CEMEX (which took over RMC), Anglo American (which owns Tarmac and BLI) and Lafarge, to both longstanding and new destinations as the customers require them.

Container traffic is in the main handled by Freightliner Intermodal, although the likes of EWS, DRS and Fastline can be seen hauling similar trains around the country as well.

As well as these bulk cargoes, EWS's 'Wagonload' network (the 'Enterprise' name has been quietly dropped it seems)

It is a great shame that in order to gain a train as externally stylish as the Pendolino, more classic, charismatic types have to make way. Although the Class 390s are rather cramped and reminiscent of budget air travel, appearing less spacious internally than the Mk 3s they were introduced to replace, their higher operating speed has brought the rail centres served closer together.

On 21 August 2004, Alstom built No 390006 *Virgin Sun* makes good time as it flashes through the rolling Cumbrian topography at Great Strickland, whilst forming the 15.35 Glasgow Central to London Euston. *Mark Darby*

handles traffic ranging in scope from china clay to car parts, pipes to paper, fertiliser to foodstuffs and salt to sugarstone, with just about everything in between.

The rationalisation of the British coal industry has been ongoing since 1913 and in recent times at least, this has led to a change in the pattern of services rather than a reduction in the number of trains run. It seems hard to believe, but in recent years deep coal mines have disappeared completely from Scotland and the last deep mine in Wales was set to close in January 2008, with just opencast or drift mining operations left to fly the flag. Therefore, the majority of power stations are now reliant on coal from port instead of pit, with the likes of Russia, South Africa, Australia and China all able to supply it more cheaply from abroad.

The steel industry too has seen continuous change with the tinplate and galvanising works at Ebbw Vale shutting completely in 2002, at the same time as the blast furnaces of Llanwern and the rolling mills of Lackenby. Rail traffic was severely affected by these changes with the loss of iron ore and coal trains between Port Talbot and Llanwern amongst numerous other flows. However, new photographic opportunities opened up instead with the introduction of long distance slab trains between Lackenby and Llanwern/Port Talbot. However, not everything lasts for ever and following increased efficiencies at Port Talbot and the introduction of imported slab through Newport Docks, even these trains seemed to have dried up.

To carry all these wonderful products around, there is a truly massive variety of industry and private owner wagons, and they too are colourful beyond belief. Here again, we have seen a considerable change from the sectorisation days when Transrail grey, Loadhaul orange & black and Mainline blue liveried wagons could be seen. Although those liveries are still around in part today, we have in addition, EWS maroon, Freightliner green, GBRf 'silver' and DRS blue, as well as a multitude of private owner liveries, far too numerous in number to even begin listing here.

## Other traffic

As well as passenger and freight trains, there are the increasingly popular test trains, brought more recently into the limelight due to the use of heritage traction in the form of Network Rail and Rail Vehicle Engineering Limited (RVEL)-owned '31s' as well as DRS 37s. The days of red and grey Serco liveried coaches hauled around by Res '47s' are long gone, replaced a few years ago by Railtrack-liveried '31s' in their lime green and blue. Today, it is more likely you will see Network Rail yellow livery on both locomotives and coaches, as the older liveries are gradually replaced by the new corporate colour scheme.

Speaking of coaches, these too provide an equally glamorous dynamic to the rail industry coming packaged in a considerable variety of different forms, ranging from the old 'Big Four' company colours of LMS maroon and GWR chocolate and cream, to BRs 'blood and custard' livery. Charter rakes too can be seen in special one-off liveries varying from green & cream to DRS blue. An assortment of former and current Train Operating Company schemes can also be captured, ranging from Virgin red to First Great Western green and Arriva Trains Wales turquoise to Wessex pink. The best thing about the latter of which that could be said, is that it did at least stand out in the landscape.

Cargo D's blue and grey stock is proving highly popular with photographers and when combined with BR blue No 86101, is sure to cause quite a stir. Now who would have thought that we would actually *want* to set eyes on a BR Blue and grey combination again, when 25 years ago, it was all that could be seen and we were, without exception, moaning about how we would like to be rid of it!

## Variety

With EWS, Freightliner, GBRf, DRS and now even Fastline all buying Class 66s, many enthusiasts bemoan the fact that there is no variety anymore. This is only true to a certain extent. The likes of the Class 40 Preservation Society, the Class 50 Association, Cotswold Rail, The Diesel Traction Group, the Harry Needle Railroad Company, Martyn Walker, Network Rail, Riviera Trains, Victa Westlink, the West Coast Railway Company, numerous private owners, and most recently Colas Rail, means that Class 20s, 31s, 33s, a '40', a '45', Class 47s, 50s, a '52', a '55', Class 56s and 73s can still be seen on the network today. The age-old tradition of enthusiasts hating the

No 47829 has the latter-day standard Cross Country rake of seven coaches in tow, pictured accelerating away from its Cheltenham stop on Friday 5 April 2002 whilst forming the 1V48 11.15 SX Manchester Piccadilly to Bristol Temple Meads.

This locomotive was unveiled in Police livery at Birmingham New Street on 25 March 2002, as part of a BTP initiative to reduce vandalism and trespass in the Midlands. It was one of six '47s' given celebrity repaints (47826 in Swallow InterCity, 47840 in BR blue, 47847 in Large Logo, 47851 in two-tone green and 47853 in XP64 were the others) in a highly commendable move by Virgin Trains, prior to the staged introduction that year of its new Voyager fleet.

The last Virgin Cross Country operated, locomotive-hauled, diesel train, used No 47851 *Traction Magazine* on the 1V45 09.16 SO Manchester Piccadilly to Paignton and 1M25 16.17 return on Saturday 21 September 2002, which the Type 4 worked to and from Birmingham New Street. The last timetabled run of 1V45/1M25, a week later, used HST power cars Nos 43097 and 43166 instead of the usual locomotive and hired in Virgin West Coast stock, to avoid alleged potential trouble on the day.
*Adrian Kenny*

'new' and lamenting the 'old' continues apace, it being as unjustified today as it was 40 years ago.

Remember that everyone, without exception, hated the 512 Brush Type 4s (Class 47s) when they were first built and yet enthusiasts chased them around half the length of the country when their days became numbered on Virgin Cross Country's services in 2002. The same applied to first generation diesel multiple-units (DMUs) and later electric multiple-units (EMUs) when it was realised that their time was coming to an end. More recent examples have included the '56s' and '58s', both of which gained something of a cult following – but only *after* EWS had announced that it was to withdraw the entire fleet of both. Similarly, Class 60s became popular all of a sudden when their numbers dipped below the quarter mark. And although this class has gained in strength over the past few years, this is mostly due to the fact that EWS has found more profitable use for its 'sheds' (Class 66s) abroad in France.

## History starts today

Whilst it is certainly true that the number of locomotive classes has dwindled, the amazing variety of liveries, new TOCs introducing new services and the constantly changing freight scene, still make British railways one of ever-changing wonderment. There were many steam locomotive photographers who hung up their cameras when it finished in 1968, who now regret not taking those Class 17 'Claytons' and Class 23 'Baby Deltics'. Despite what many may think, it is the same today. Many are hanging up their cameras and turning to overseas for entertainment now that, for instance, Voyagers and Pendolinos have replaced '47s' and '87s'. However, with the current Voyager livery already on the way to becoming history, how many will regret in the future not having a balanced record of Virgin's red and silver scheme running around the country? It is worth bearing in mind that when the 309 Class 37s were first introduced, they were disliked in much a similar way as the Voyagers and Pendolinos are today. And yet today, we witness people travelling hundreds of miles to ride behind or photograph the few remaining examples of these locomotives, which are now looked upon with something approaching reverence. The photographic history of the early diesels is much the poorer for people deciding that the hobby had become boring once steam finished and it is hoped that at least some of the present day enthusiasts will see the light and record what is there today, '66s' included, for future generations to come.

## Conclusion

To conclude our journey around Great Britain, we would like to explain that in our attempts to make the liveries and operations we have recorded as diverse as possible, there may be a slight bias towards certain geographical areas or routes. This is purely a consequence of the frequency of trains on particular lines at a given time and therefore merely mirrors contemporary traffic volume. Similarly, we are acutely aware that there are numerous liveries (mostly one-offs) and even two locomotive classes (can you see which ones?) 'missing' from the book. However, we have also included a few classes that might surprise the reader, such as an '03', a '24', and a 'Warship'! Therefore it needs to be explained that we have chosen only what we consider to be high quality photos, rather than 'shoe-horn' in a photo that may be of an inferior quality, just to represent a particular class or livery. We hope you understand.

The number of liveries in this book is open to interpretation, for instance, should the silver of the Corus 60 be counted as different from the silver of the EWS 67, and/or should an unbranded Virgin livery be counted as separate to a fully branded version and/or should the silver branding on a GNER livery be counted as different from the later gold version? After some considerable thought, we feel that the brandings and colours represent different time periods and different stages in the evolution of the railways and therefore, for the sake of argument, we have for the purposes of this book, counted them as separate. Having said that, we have counted Porterbrook's purple livery on the Class 47, 57 and 87 as one, the reason being, that even though they are considerably different from each other, the difference is purely because of the type of locomotive, rather than a change in ownership or time period. Therefore, after several counts, we deem that the 130 photographs on display here, show some 71 liveries on 37 different classes of locomotive and unit.

Although this book is intended to show as many of the different locomotives and liveries as possible, we have also attempted to show the wide variety of coaching stock combinations and freight miscellany that can be seen on the network today. It should be noted that the livery 'count' does not include these coaching stock or wagon variations and so this should go even further to adding distinctiveness and variety to the book. We sincerely hope that this will go some way to offset the oft-stated and entirely erroneous 'there is no variety anymore'.

There are literally thousands of livery combinations that can be achieved between locomotive and coach/wagon and this book barely scratches the surface of the quite amazing kaleidoscope of colours that can be viewed on the system today.

## Technical details

All of the photographs presented were exposed on Fuji Provia film, mainly 100ASA, but with some 400ASA and Tungsten 64ASA shots as well. The prime equipment has been that of Mamiya 645 medium format cameras coupled to a selection of Sekor lenses, with the remainder of the photographs taken by a Pentax 6x7 married to Takumar optics. Although pleasing 'contre jour' effects and images can be obtained in all weathers, we have felt that the best medium to show off the different liveries in this book is that of sunshine and we have endeavoured to find and reproduce only such images here. However, to offer some variety and a bit of relief, there is the occasional 'off the wall' or night shot – after all, black is still a colour.

With the advent of digital photography along with the opportunity to 'doctor' images at home, we would like to emphasise that all photographs contained within this volume actually happened on the day, and that other than a small amount of cropping, no enhancement or manipulation has been carried out in any way.

## Thanks

Thanks must go to Tom Ferris and Peter Waller at Ian Allan for the blank canvas and the encouragement. Thanks must also be extended to the various railwaymen, contacts and 'gen men' within the industry for their help and information, without which, many of these workings would have gone unrecorded. Finally, the important bit; thanks must go to our long-suffering wives, Carolyn, Caron and Jane for their patience, understanding and support of our many hours at the line side, when we could have been doing something better around the house! Further thanks are due to Roger Smith for his help in tracking down information for some of the captions and to Jane for doing the majority of the initial typing.

*Mark Darby, Paul Higgins, Neil Higson and Adrian Kenny*

The light and shade over Dentdale on the magnificent Settle & Carlisle line presented an alluring panoramic vista on 21 August 2004, as No 66250, the final English Welsh & Scottish Railway (EWS) example of this ubiquitous General Motors product, headed over the 591ft-long Dent Head Viaduct hauling 6E24, the 06.20 Ayr Falkland Yard to Milford Junction. The train will shortly plunge into 7,887ft of darkness as Blea Moor Tunnel is negotiated. In the distance, above the 10th wagon the lonely outpost of Dent station can be made out. The reign of these American imports began with the unloading of No 66001 at Immingham docks on the morning of Saturday 18 April 1998. This spelt the end for traditional types as the cull of older machines began in earnest in November of that year. *Mark Darby*

Friday 6 June 2006 sees Nos 50049/031, masquerading as 50012/28, thunder past Wickwar with the 'Orcadian' (1Z27, 06.40 Swindon to Inverness) railtour. On arrival at the Highland capital, the charter continued that weekend to Kyle of Lochalsh and Wick/Thurso, eventually returning South on the Monday. The train has just passed through the site of Wickwar station, which closed to goods on 10 June 1963 and passengers on 4 January 1965 after 121 years serving this small Gloucestershire town.

The two immaculate Class 50 Alliance locomotives have had an exciting life since entering preservation in 1992, having worked in most parts of the UK, including locations never visited by the class when in BR revenue service. With the locomotives beautifully prepared in large logo livery, it was a great shame such a motley collection of different-liveried coaches were assembled for this high profile tour. *Neil Higson*

Network Rail owned, operated and liveried No 31105 in yellow (nearest) and privately owned, Fragonset Merlin Rail (FMR)-operated, Serco-crewed and Railtrack-liveried No 31190 *Gryphon* are captured under the magnificent roof of Bristol Temple Meads, whilst sandwiching Ultrasonic Test Unit 2 on Thursday 20 January 2005, forming 4Z08, the 18.55 St Phillips Marsh to Tyseley test train. Soon after this photograph was taken, No 31190 received a coat of maroon paint and was hired to the West Coast Railway Company to work as required on that season's

'Royal Scotsman' programme. However, the maroon livery did not last long either and the locomotive is now resplendent in BR green, having gained this latest livery at the end of 2006. No 31190 is still privately owned but, along with Nos 31106 and 31459, is now run by Rail Vehicle Engineering, transferring to this company's fleet in January 2007 when FMR went into administration. *Adrian Kenny*

The only operator on the national network to employ Class 56s at the business end of its trains is Fastline Freight. It has re-introduced three former EWS locomotives to traffic. Two examples, Nos 56045 and 56124 became Nos 56301 and 56302 respectively after expensive overhauls by Brush at Loughborough, while No 56125 became 56303 after a refettle by FM Rail at Derby with this locomotive leased to Fastline, rather than owned by the company. The first working of the re-invigorated 'Grids' commenced in March 2006.

On 20 November 2006, No 56302 pounds through Portway, near Tamworth with 4O90, the 11.01 Doncaster Hexthorp to Grain. In the early days this train ran virtually empty. However, current loadings are far healthier and this service now runs two days a week from Doncaster and three from Birch Coppice. *Paul Higgins*

On 17 August 2006 one of the final active EWS Class 37s, No 37405 approaches Hampden Park with a mixed rake of Pullman stock forming 1Z28, the 17.12 Eastbourne to Bristol Temple Meads; Kingfisher Tours' returning 'Sunny Seaside Spitfire', which was run in conjunction with Eastbourne's seafront air show. The '37' was deputising for the originally advertised, but then unavailable, 'Battle of Britain' 4-6-2 No 34067 *Tangmere*. The circuitous return route through South London, via Norwood, Clapham Junction, Acton Wells and the Western Region main line gave the diehard 'tractor' fans on board more than five hours of heritage haulage to look forward to.

Beyond Hampden Park lies Willingdon Junction, where the Brighton and Hastings routes diverge. Until the late 1970s this was the southerly junction of a triangle (Polegate East Junction and Stone Cross Junction) constructed by the London, Brighton & South Coast Railway to facilitate through running directly between Brighton and Hastings. Prior to becoming an electric train heat (ETH) example, previous incarnations of this locomotive were D6982 and 37282. The name *Strathclyde Region* was carried between April 1986 and May 1997. *Mark Darby*

One of eight High Speed Train (HST) power cars converted in 1987/88 at Derby and Stratford for use with Class 91s on the East Coast main line (ECML), buffer and draw gear-fitted No 43065 passes through Millbrook, Southampton, with an unidentified Cross Country working on 21 April 1997.

The modified power cars were used as surrogate Driving Van Trailers (DVTs), initially only supplying the power for the train's auxiliaries but as the power cars were idling most of the time, engine problems soon began to arise and so were soon modified to supply traction power.

With the Class 91 also supplying the traction via Time Division Multiplex (TDM) equipment fitted in the power cars, the HST formation gave an impressive 8000hp! The operation commenced in March 1988, running between Kings Cross and Leeds but by late 1988 enough Mk 4 coaches and DVTs were available to allow the power car back to normal use.

After Virgin had finished with No 43065, it went into store for a number of years but is now active again on its former home turf, painted in black and working between Sunderland and Kings Cross for Grand Central. *Neil Higson*

There are no less than six people in this view of No 60038, although one of them is more implied than actually visible! Can you spot them all?

The locomotive has brought 16 BCA and BLAs of coil up from Margam via the Ogmore Vale extension line and is seen amongst the still-surviving semaphores at Tondu. The train is the 6M30 11.10 SunO Margam TC to Dee Marsh Sidings, diverted this way due to engineering works on the main line. It is Sunday 12 March 2000 and on this date, trains were unusually being run round using the Llynfi Valley line to Maesteg instead of the more usual Garw loop, which curves sharply off to the right. The locomotive has completed its run-round manoeuvre and is seen about to give up the token to the signalman, before proceeding down to Bridgend and the mainline eastwards. *Adrian Kenny*

After Virgin Cross Country ceased locomotive-hauled trains in favour of the rather claustrophobic Voyager fleet, the small stud of repainted celebrity Brush Type 4s were left hauling electric powered stock on diversions away from energised routes. These services are popularly known amongst the enthusiast fraternity as 'Drags'.

On 1 September 2002, only a few weeks after the Class 47s' regular work had ceased, No 47853 Rail Express passes the entrance to Hams Hall freight terminal at Whitacre Junction with a diverted Wolverhampton to Euston express, which on this date, due to track upgrades on the Southern section of the West Coast main line, was booked to terminate at Milton Keynes. No 47853 is a true celebrity in every sense of the word. It carried the light blue XP64 blue livery to match the experimental XP64 carriage stock when delivered in 1964 as D1733. Before receiving its '47/8' classification the numbers 47141 and 47614 were also carried. The name Rail Express was unveiled at a ceremony at Grosmont on the North Yorkshire Moors Railway by the magazine's editors Phil Sutton and Murray Brown, along with Chris Green, the Chief Executive of Virgin Trains on 27 April 2002. Paul Higgins

A fine carpet of rosebay willowherb leads the viewer's eye towards Mirlees 8MB 275T-powered No 60007, one of only four 'Tugs' to receive Loadhaul black and orange colours. The others were Nos 60008, 038 and 059. Photographed on 31 July 2001, the Immingham-based machine powers through Bhessie Ghyll on the northern climbs of the West Coast main line, running two hours early with 6E41 the 19.43 Hardendale Quarry to Tyne Yard. The wagons are colloquially known as the 'white ladies', and convey lime for the steel making process. The 'covhops' at the front of the train will be destined for Lackenby, where as the open tops behind are bound for Redcar. *Mark Darby*

A glorious 2 May 1999 sees Nos 37250 and 73138 blast out of the 819yd Bincombe Tunnel near Dorchester with the second of two runs that day from Yeovil Junction to Weymouth Quay, the 1Z95 14.20 departure from Yeovil. This trip proved to be the penultimate train down the Quay branch, only a Sandite diesel-electric multiple-unit running thereafter, and due to 'maintenance issues' the line's future is at best uncertain.

No 37250 was one of 42 Class 37s to be exported to France in 1999, departing UK shores on 16 July 1999, to assist with the building of the high speed LGV Méditerranée line between Saint-Marcel-lès-Valence and Marseille. Since its return to the UK on 16 Sept 2000, it has sat rotting in Tyne Yard.

As for 73138, it was lucky to escape the scrapyard after its withdrawal in Sept 1999 and is currently stored at Long Marston in an operational condition, being owned by the AC Loco Group.
*Neil Higson*

One of the more unusual moves of 2006 was the introduction by Arriva Trains Wales, in August, of a 46-year-old, Class 121 'bubble car' to work the Cardiff Bay-Cardiff Queen Street shuttle service. It performs this roughly 1 mile, 3minute trip, eight times an hour, almost every hour, six days a week, between 06.42 and 23.49, making a total of 138 trips and covering 147 miles 53 chains every working day, plus another 2 miles and 24 chains in empty carriage stock (ECS) moves – more than all three of the former Rhymney Class 37 diagrams combined! Under setting skies, and with the piped end leading, No 121032 is seen residing in Cardiff Bay station on Saturday 3 February 2007, having worked in as 2B92, the 17.57 from Cardiff Queen Street and waiting to form 2S98, the 18.04 back out again. *Adrian Kenny*

Despite being between 40 and 50 years old, Class 20s can still be seen on the main line today with both DRS and the Harry Needle Railroad Company owning several examples. The latter owner's pair Nos 20905 and 20096 are seen at Evesham on Saturday 17 December 2006 on temporary hire to Cotswold Rail, to haul ex-Virgin stock No's 43121, 40419, 44021 and 43158 to Long Marston for storage, as the 5Z22 08.52 from Gloucester. Long Marston has seen a revival in fortunes during 2006 and 2007, being used as secure storage for all sorts of off-lease stock. The Long Marston branch has also seen Mainline Rail and Cotswold '31s' a Nemesis Rail Class 33, hauling dead '56s', EWS '37s' a DRS '37', an FMR '45', a Freightliner '47', Riviera '47s' Cotswold, '47s' in abundance, a Cotswold '57' an EWS '60' EWS '66', DRS '66s' GB Railfreight (GBRf) '66s' and even a South West Trains '73', ex Virgin and ex-Anglia '86s' and former Cotswold, GBRf, and Virgin Class '87s', albeit hauled dead. There was even a brief period of revenue-earning freight with FMR Class 47s towards the end of 2006, taking auctioned cars to and fro between Long Marston and Mossend. *Adrian Kenny*

The normally uninspiring fens of Cambridgeshire woke briefly in the summer of 2004 to the sound of diesel-hauled passenger trains. This occurred whilst work was carried out in Ipswich Tunnel to facilitate the passage of larger containers, this occupation taking place between mid-July and early September. On the extremely hot morning of 4 September, the diverted 1G19 07.51 SO Norwich to London Liverpool Street approaches the River Ouse at Stretham behind the former *S.S. Great Britain* No 47813, with No 90007 dead in tow. The beautiful Ely Cathedral can be made out above the rear of the train. Liveried in First Great Western green, No 47813 has carried three previous identities, D1720, 47129 and 47658. No 90007 has only carried one number, but two names; it was originally named *Lord Stamp* at Euston on 1 April 1992, the former Virgin machine became *Keith Harpur* in September 2002. This name was subsequently removed and bestowed upon No 87031 in 2004. *Mark Darby*

Within its class, No 92031 *The Institute of Logistics and Transport* is almost unique, but not quite. Amongst the 46 6760hp Class 92s (their output whilst operating under 25kV AC conditions), only No 92001 *Victor Hugo* supports EWS's red and gold colour scheme. The remaining 45 class members are still anonymously liveried in the bland two-tone grey colours in which they were delivered. When Class 92s draw the 'juice' from the former Southern Region's 750V dc third rail, their output is reduced slightly to 5360hp. However, this would not have disadvantaged No 92031 on 4 April 2003, as it forged south, beneath the wires at Great Brington with a colourful rake of containers and tanks, forming 4Z50, the 09.15 Trafford Park-Purfleet. *Paul Higgins*

No 60033 *Tees Steel Express* storms past Brinkworth near Wootton Bassett hauling 6B33, the 13.25 Theale to Robeston discharged TEA/TDA fuel tanks in the distinctive old red, white and blue and new all-over red Murco colours. The service to Theale has been running for many years, initially with single Class 47 power but with extra wagons being added to the consist, pairs of Class 37s became the norm from 1988. By the early 1990s the use of Class 60s had increased the trailing load to 24 of the 100-tonne tanks.

No 60033 entered service on 22 February 1991 and was initially a Trainload Petroleum locomotive, named *Anthony Ashley Cooper*. In July 1997 it was one of two to be selected and painted in the British Steel bright blue colours, and subsequently was renamed. With Corus taking over British Steel, by November 2000 a repaint into the new company's house colours of silver had been completed, looking striking but prone to showing the grime! *Neil Higson*

On the morning of 14 August 2003 the North East coast line at Hunt Cliff reverberates to the sound of a recently reinstated No 56033 *Shotton Paper Mill* powering a rake of empties to the top of the hill before the engine is shut off and it descends down to Crag Hall signalbox and onward to its journey's end at the Cleveland potash mine in Boulby. Here the wagons will be reloaded with potash for a return to Tees Dock to be loaded on to a ship for export. The background of the photograph is the industrial landscape of Redcar and Teesside where the return working will end up. Since the photograph was taken EWS has operated Class 60 and 66 locomotives on these trains, but since mid-2007, Freightliner has taken over these operations using its own Class 66s. This has had the knock-on effect of a large scale downgrade in activity at the EWS depot at Thornaby. *Paul Higgins*

Introduced into traffic as E6043 on 11 September 1966, No 73136 had at the time of this photograph recently returned to the national network in original condition, albeit supporting *Perseverance* nameplates. On the first day of April 2006 it was captured on film near Falmer, bringing the unusual sight of a locomotive-hauled train on the line from Lewes to Brighton, whilst hauling 1Z73, the 09.35 London Cannon Street to Littlehampton 'Blueberry Fool' railtour. This trip was routed via Hastings, Eastbourne and Brighton, also visiting the branch lines to Seaford and Bognor Regis. This tour was run jointly by Hertfordshire Railtours and Fragonset Merlin. *Mark Darby*

On 28 October 1996 the worst storms in living memory battered the town of Minehead. By morning severe damage had been done to the sea defences with the town left under 3ft of water! The repair plan called for a large quantity of limestone boulders, with rail the chosen means of transporting these from the Mendip quarries. After a search for spare wagons by EWS, the decrepit YCV 'Turbots' were chosen. Refurbishment, which included a repaint from rust to EWS maroon at Perth was soon under way, with the initial train running on 24 March 1997.

The daily (M-F) train, 8Z90 13.15 Merehead to Minehead is seen passing the delightful station at Washford on the West Somerset Railway on 15 May 1997, with its load of boulders. No 37894 in obsolete Trainload Coal livery was just one of a large number of different '37s' in varying liveries to work the train, with occasional '33s', '47s' and even a preserved diesel-hydraulic Class 52 also putting in an appearance! Eventually, 106,000 tonnes of stone were delivered by 235 trains over a 15-month period. *Neil Higson*

EWS had the contract to provide power for the 'Royal Scotsman' trains, until it was taken over by the West Coast Railway Company for the 2005 season onwards. Here, Nos 37197 *Loch Laidon* and 37261 *Loch Arkaig* make a superb sight and an even better sound, blasting out of Bridge of Orchy on the fantastic summer's evening of Saturday 6 August 2005. The train is 1H95, the 13.40 Edinburgh to Spean Bridge and is on day one of its four-day 'Western' tour to Mallaig, Taynuilt and Wemyss Bay. *Adrian Kenny*

The imposing outline of the former Battersea power station forms an unmistakeable backdrop, which is a far cry from the more modern glass and steel buildings that now dominate a vast amount of London's skyline.

Although slightly out of the time span in question, 'Cromptons' (as they were colloquially known due to their Crompton Parkinson electrical equipment) were still very much part of the everyday South London suburban network which was their spiritual home. On 26 June 1994,

'Dutch' liveried *Shakespeare Cliff*, the former No D6569, ambles up to a signal check at Wandsworth Road, with a short rake of YDA 'Octopus' Skako Bogie Ballast Hopper wagons. Shakespeare Cliff is that it is the location where the Channel Tunnel exits the United Kingdom. The locomotive was named on 16 May 1988, along with No 33050 *Isle of Grain* at Trans Manche Link's terminal on the Isle of Grain. No 33051 was withdrawn in August 1998, with cutting up taking place at Eastleigh depot in the first week of October 2003. *Paul Higgins*

Exceptionally clear light illuminated Teesside on 15 February 2003, as 60083 *Mountsorrel* headed away from Newport East junction with 6V37, the 12.59 Lackenby to Llanwern 'lumps', formed of BBA steel carriers. These wagons have corrugated bases to dissipate heat and to aid loading by fork lift trucks. Both of Middlesborough's landmark bridges which span the River Tees can be

seen, most prominent is the lifting bridge, and on the horizon, the transporter bridge. Named by Mrs Rosemary Robson, wife of the LaFarge Redland aggregates rail manager, 60083 became *Mountsorrel* at Toton traction depot on 30 August 1998. *Mark Darby*

No 47810 makes a welcome change from the usual HST services as it climbs the 1 in 330 gradient through the site of Box station, shut in 1965, with 1E33, the 11.10 Bristol Temple Meads–Newcastle on Saturday 17 October 1998. This Virgin Cross Country service was diverted off its booked route due to engineering work in North Bristol. It is about to enter the 198yd Middle Hill Tunnel, which precedes Box Tunnel on the Bath-Wootton Bassett route. This section of Brunel's London to Bristol line was the last to open due to the difficulty in cutting the 1 in 100 gradient through the 1mile 1,452yd Box Tunnel, which, when the Great Western Line finally opened on 30 June 1841, became the longest rail tunnel in the world.

Built in March 1964, No 47810 can today be seen in its Cotswold livery and a *Captain Sensible* nameplate. As D1924 back in July 1967, its moment of fame was hauling the final 'Bournemouth Belle' to Waterloo on the last day of steam on the Southern Region. In December 1973 it became No 47247, before ETH fitting led to its being renumbered 47655. *Neil Higson*

**Opposite:** The movement of gritstone from South Wales to various destinations all over the country has been one of the successful freight stories of the past 10 years. Gritstone is a generic name given to the aggregate used in the surface course of roads all over the country. Its resistance to the constant wear of traffic makes it a highly sought after product.

Gritstone from Aggregate Industries (AI) Cwm Nant Lleici Quarry north of Pontardawe is loaded on to rail at Neath Abbey Wharf, or Neath AWF for short. Trains from Neath AWF run initially to Pengam sidings in Cardiff, where they then recess for a few hours until forming a train to either Angerstein Wharf, Thorney Mill, Harlow Mill, Tavistock Junction, Burngullow or Theale depending on customer requirements.

No 66530 hauling 35 VTG-owned PGAs is seen on the first leg of this journey, the 6B75 12.38 'Q' Neath AWF to Pengam, crossing the 150yd Neath River Viaduct on Monday 6 November 2006, with the stone on this occasion eventually destined for Thorney Mill. *Adrian Kenny*

What would we give today for a large logo blue Class 47 with a silver roof and black head code box in full sun? The answer is a bridge full of photographers with mobile phones tracking its every move. On 8 July 1994 I stood on my own to photograph No 47674 *Women's Royal Voluntary Service* which was headed south down the Midland main line passing Finedon Road Sidings. This was a regular train, the 5001 York Works to Strawberry Hill depot in South London, conveying two brand new Class 465 Networker units for Network SouthEast commuter services.

As can be seen from the rusty tracks in the foreground the busy times of the yard are long past. Only redundant stored coal wagons have recently spent time here prior to being scrapped. Today the area is once again busy with GBRf using a newly laid yard to prepare and assemble Metronet infrastructure trains that head to London's underground network at weekends. The engine is active today, but has lost its blue livery in favour of West Coast Railways maroon with small yellow ends. It has also been renumbered as 47854. *Paul Higgins*

For several months in Spring 2006, whilst repairs were carried out on Leven Viaduct, where the former Furness route crosses Cartmel Sands near Ulverston, all nuclear flask traffic was using the northern stretch of the Cumbrian coast line. One of the diverted trains, 6C51 the 10.17 Sellafield to Heysham is seen skirting the Cumbrian coast to the south of Workington behind DRS Nos 37606 and 37607 on 31 May. Both locomotives have carried three previous identities; No 37606 began life as D6790, changing under TOPS to 37090; after receiving a new alternator and re-geared CP7 bogies, it became No 37508. No 37607 also became a re-geared '37/5'; No 37511 after carrying D6803 and 37103. The '37/6' concept was originally a refurbishment for the haulage of Nightstar stock which turned out to be an expensive white elephant! *Mark Darby*

The Far North line is one of the lesser photographed lines in the UK due to its lack of traffic variety and its remoteness from the rest of Britain. This is a pity, as it does offer some rich rewards for the patient (and lucky) enthusiast. After a gap of many years, freight traffic on the line resumed on 29 September 1995 but it was not until 6 April 2000 that daily trains commenced with a portion off the Inverness 'Safeway Flyer', conveying swap body containers onwards to Georgemas Junction for Safeway stores at Alness, Thurso, Wick, Kirkwall and the Orkney Isles.

In 2003, there was also a roughly weekly train of materials for Thurso Building Supplies and a return flow of refrigerators from the Norfrost factory at Castleton to Leyland and later Rugby, both in VKA vans. Here No 66112 with two empty Safeway containers and two loaded VKA vans forms the 4D66 11.28 Georgemas Junction to Mossend on Wed 3 Sept 2003, running through the highly pleasant Strath of Kildonan.

Owing to a combination of the Safeway stores in Scotland being taken over by Morrisons and EWS abruptly suspending its intermodal trains, all three of these services ceased to run in 2004 and have not returned. *Adrian Kenny*

In true East Coast main line sleekness and style, the unique No 89001 (nicknamed 'The Badger' due to its sloping nose) storms north at Essendine, Lincolnshire, bearing its immaculate dark GNER blue with red pin stripe. It is seen working its regular Saturday afternoon 14.30 Kings Cross to Leeds turn on 16 May 1998.

The BREL Crewe-built locomotive, new in 1986, was designed as a prototype for passenger and freight work, but after testing, BR decided on the Class 91 and fixed formation rakes as the best option for the ECML. Named *Avocet* at Sandy, Bedfordshire in September 1989 by the then Prime Minister Margaret Thatcher, it was stored in July 1992 and passed into the hands of a group of Brush employees who looked after it.

In 1997 it was returned to mainline operation as cover for GNER whilst Class 91 locomotives were overhauled. Today the engine is again preserved, at Barrow Hill by the AC Locomotive Group which has returned it to its original InterCity executive colours. *Paul Higgins*

No 47813 leaves a faint wisp of Sulzer exhaust behind as it storms through Thetford Forest, at Santon Downham, heading the Saturdays-Only 1G20, the 11.24 London Liverpool Street to Great Yarmouth on 4 September 2004. No 90001, which had powered the train from Liverpool Street, was still attached, out of sight at the rear, and would stay in the formation to the Norfolk resort. The train is passing lineside paraphernalia of a bygone era, namely telegraph poles ... still supporting wires! No 9720, the Driving Brake Standard Open coupled next to the locomotive was the sole recipient of 'One' livery, painted only as insurance against a Mk 3 Driving Van Trailer not receiving the relevant paperwork in time for the official 'One' launch on 1 April 2004. 'One' is an acronym for 'Operated by National Express'. *Mark Darby*

This barren view at Onllwyn on 2 September 1996 depicts Nos 37889 and 37896, both Welsh machines for most of their 40-year careers pushing the 6Z35 Aberthaw-Onllwyn back into the washery for loading. Both built in early 1964, the locomotives were formerly No 37231, which was scrapped at Crewe on 23 March 2007 and No 37233, which at the time of writing was dumped at Margam. The HDA hopper wagons, built at Shildon in 1982, were the final 460 from a production run of more than 10,000. They have upgraded brake cylinders so as to allow 60mph running when loaded, initially for long distance flows, but were found to be useful on the steeply graded Welsh branches where the additional brake force was most welcome. Onllwyn Washery, on an isolated South Wales hilltop, was once home to four drifts, employing hundreds of men, but now currently washes approximately 900,000 tonnes of coal a year for both the domestic and foreign markets. The coal is brought in by lorries from local opencast mines such as the Nant Helen, then railed out when blended, Aberthaw power station being the main user. The washery is expected to be in operation for another 10 years. *Neil Higson*

Some of the more elusive services to run in Britain, are the various track testing trains operated by Serco for Network Rail. However, the colourful nature of these trains means that the hard work and persistence in trying to track down their movements is (mostly!) worthwhile in the end.

Rail express systems-liveried No 47781 *Isle of Iona* and No 47749 *Atlantic College* 'top and tail' the Track Inspection Train, the 1Z12 08.05 Swansea to Derby Railway Technical Centre, running initially via Aberthaw to Cardiff (reverse), then back via Aberthaw to Bridgend (reverse) and then east again via Pontyclun to Cardiff, Gloucester and Derby. The well-maintained location is St Georges on the South Wales main line and the date is Friday 15 August 2003. *Adrian Kenny*

More than 20 years have elapsed since the Lammermuirs echoed to the beautifully orchestrated symphony produced by the Napier 'Deltics' as they plied their trade at the head of Anglo-Scottish expresses. Seven years after British Rail retired the majestic Class 55s, British Rail Engineering Limited (BREL) unveiled the 'Young Pretender' in the form of the Class 91, on 12 February 1988, at Crewe Works.

Bombardier commenced overhauls of the class in 2000, and the doyen member, No 91001 *City of London* became 91101, photographed in its GNER 'Stealth Bomber' blue livery, passing Houndwood in the Scottish Lowlands, on 31 May 2005, leading a Kings Cross-Edinburgh Waverley service. *Paul Higgins*

'4CEP' No 2311 trundles past the site of the former Royal Navy cordite factory at Holton Bay with the 10.59 Wareham-Brockenhurst stopping service on 12 January 2005. Class 412 No 2311 was one of 22 '4BEP' buffet units built to work with the popular '4CEP' slam-door units on the Kent Coast electrification scheme of the late 1950s, being based at Ramsgate. Built at Eastleigh in 1961 as unit 7019, refurbishment came in late 1982 at Swindon Works and on release was reallocated to Fratton for use on the South Western Division. In September 2002 it lost its buffet vehicle, this replaced by a Trailer Standard Open from a withdrawn 'CEP' and was renumbered 2311, technically making it a '4CEP'.

In its last few years it moved around the Southern, ending its days working out of Waterloo for South West Trains. On 14 March 2005, a short circuit in the Driving Motor Standard Open whilst working 1B68, the 18.55 Southampton Central-Waterloo, caused its demise after 44 years' service!

Luckily preservation beckoned, and on 6 April 2005 it was towed to the Eden Valley Railway at Warcop in Cumbria, by GBRf No 66711. *Neil Higson*

The sole unbranded Loadhaul-liveried Class 37, No 37516, appeared well 'off' region on 4 August 1998, as it accelerated away from Eastleigh station with a train composed of Sealion and Seacow hoppers, forming the 7B05 10.35 Eastleigh Yard to Southampton Western Docks. Two of the hoppers had recently been outshopped in EWS house colours. The stone to be collected had been shipped from Foster Yeoman's remote Glensanda Quarry in the North West of Scotland.

In the background No 58010 sits in the down platform road, having returned after working 6B43, the Tuesdays-Only Fawley tanks. Loadhaul, formed in 1994, was formerly known as Trainload Freight North. Originally numbered D6786, No 37516 became a recipient of CP7 bogies and replacement alternator, having been renumbered to 37086 when the TOPS scheme was enacted. *Mark Darby*

With around one hundred years service between them, Nos 20311 and 20309, belonging to Direct Rail Services and based at Carlisle Kingmoor depot, are shown working the 7M53 12.58 Bridgwater to Crewe Basford Hall nuclear flask service, the train's ultimate destination being Sellafield reprocessing plant in Cumbria.

The flask will have started its long journey by road at Hinkley Point Power Station on the North Somerset coast. After travelling through the narrow country lanes and back streets of Bridgwater, it is transferred by crane to the 1980s-built FNA wagon.

It's 14 August 2001 and the train is seen about midway through its journey at Ryecroft Junction, Walsall, leaving the Sutton Park freight line and joining the Cannock Chase route. At this time it was still an operational requirement for the train to be made up with a barrier wagon either end of the flask carrier, but the use of the guards van had been deemed unnecessary, and the guard was relegated to the back cab! Thankfully Class 20 and 37 engines still work most of these workings today. *Paul Higgins*

The Hunslet-Barclay Class 20s will be fondly remembered by all those who witnessed the annual weedkilling campaign of the late 1980s and 1990s. The Kilmarnock-based company would supply a pair of these vintage locomotives for the Nomix-Chipman and Schering weed killing trains. These two trains would then move their way round the country in 'top and tail' mode spraying the vegetation from Penzance to Thurso and every branch line in-between!

It is 17 April 1996 and the Nomix-Chipman weed tour had reached Bristol after spending the first week of the season blitzing the vegetation of Devon and Cornwall. This specialist train, which had started operation in 1927, whistles towards Westerleigh, on the remains of the former Midland main line to Bristol, running as 7Z07 07.10 Swindon-Swindon with No 20904 *Janis* and No 20901 *Nancy* on the rear.

The last season for the 'Killer 20s' as they became known, was 1998, after which operation moved over to Multi-Purpose Vehicles (MPVs) or EWS locomotives. The six engines, all named after female staff at Hunslet-Barclay, were initially sold to DRS early in 1999, before moving to other operators. *Neil Higson*

At almost 19.00 on 28 May 2006 one of the additional but uncommon locomotive-hauled summer dated extras trundles away from Blatchbridge Junction, heading for Frome, behind Fragonset's black liveried No 31459 *Cerberus*. The train is formed by a uniform rake of 'Heart of Wessex' branded pink-liveried Mk 2s which make up 2V89, the 17.16 Weymouth to Bristol Temple Meads. The formation is tailed by matching No 31601 *The Mayor of Casterbridge*, an apt name for the route. A potted history of these '31s' saw 31601 as originally D5609 and then No 31186. No 31459 started out in life as D5684 and was then 31256. Fragonset had a memorable naming policy. Particularly noteworthy was the choice of mythological creatures, Cerberus being 'the three-headed watchdog who guarded the entrance to the lower world'. Interestingly, whilst being a regular performer topping and tailing services on the Marston Vale route, No 31601 carried the name *Bletchley Park Station X* to honour the World War 2 establishment where the Enigma code-breaking machine was devised to decipher critical German messages. *Mark Darby*

Without doubt, the most salubrious ECS to run on the national network is the stock of the Royal Train, seen here climbing away from Northampton towards Roade cutting. On 16 October 2003, dedicated Royal 'Duff', No 47798 *Prince William* in claret livery, was rostered to return the stock from a Royal engagement on Humberside, to its home at Wolverton. Due to the sensitive nature of the train, specific details of workings are always awkward to obtain.

Introduced into traffic in February 1965 as D1656, three further identities have been carried, namely 47072, 47609 *Firefly* and 47834, prior to elevation to regal status. The locomotive received the Prince's name on 8 May 1994, without ceremony at Crewe Diesel traction depot. *Paul Higgins*

Many industrial locations hire in shunters to work trains around their works or facilities. One such location in South Wales is Machen Quarry, which over the years has had Planet, Sentinel and Class 03 and 08 shunters to its name.

Here, D2199, withdrawn from Barrow shed in 1972 without ever having carried its TOPS number of 03199, runs round 10 Network Rail HQA ballast hoppers on Sunday 19 March 2006. The wagons were brought up by none other than Nos 37670 *St. Blazey T&RS Depo*t and 37669 which had worked their first trip since reinstatement over the Heart of Wales line the previous night, dropping ballast as required by the engineer. The locomotives had gone back to East Usk to pick up another 10 wagons for loading during which time, D2199 'burst' in spectacular fashion by dumping all of its oil. Thus the part-loaded first portion and empty second portion were returned to Alexandra Dock Junction by the '37s'. The '03' was later returned to the South Yorkshire Railway and replaced by No 08296 from Whatley Quarry. *Adrian Kenny*

**Opposite:** No 66100, a Motherwell-based Radio Electronic Token Block (RETB)-fitted machine, passes Clachnaharry in the Inverness suburbs with 4H30 the 18.43 Inverness-Kinbrace on a beautiful 5 August day in 2004. The trainload of OTA timber empties only worked as required, depending on what logs had been left at Kinbrace, which is situated 118 miles north of Inverness on the Far North line. There is no siding at this remote location so the train went up after the last passenger of the day. It then stopped in section to allow for lineside loading overnight, and when completed would continue seven miles further north to Forsinaird to run around and return south.

After obtaining a track access grant, EWS ran the service between 2002 and 2005, its demise being down to cost implications. Transporting Forestry Commission timber to Inverness mainly for board manufacturer Norbord, which has a factory at Dalcross near Inverness, the train, at its peak, could handle 15,000 tonnes per annum. The scheme won a national award in 2003 which recognised its development potential for Scotland's rural environment. *Neil Higson*

Over the years, the picturesque harbour at Cockwood has played host to the most auspicious classes of diesel locomotive, namely 'Westerns', 'Warships', Class 50s, 'Peaks', Brush Type 4s, 'Baby Warships', 'Cromptons' and Class 25s. Even the odd Hymek has also graced the well-known West Country causeway. In modern times, Voyagers have become the regular performers. Back in 2004, the year of this photograph, it would have seemed unthinkable that the Virgin Cross Country Voyager would no longer be operated by Virgin, however by the autumn of 2007, Arriva had won the franchise, and the distinctive trademark red and silver brandings began to disappear. Devon contains many popular holiday destinations, so it comes as no surprise that families can be seen enjoying a spot of crabbing at the waters edge, on 28 August, as the 17.35 Paignton-Manchester Piccadilly rushes past in the shape of 'Super Voyager' No 221114 *Sir Francis Drake*. *Mark Darby*

No book covering the British mainland in the past 10 years would really be complete without a picture of 'The Rhymneys'. Following tests, rugby internationals and opening ceremonies, booked locomotive haulage on the Cardiff to Rhymney corridor commenced on Monday 25 September 1995 with Pete Waterman's No 47488 *Davies the Ocean*.

There followed periods of Class 33 and 50 haulage, during which time EWS '37s' ran as well. Class 37s then took over operation of these trains completely from January 1999 and depending on the contract at the time, ran between one and three trains a day for the next six years.

In the summer of 2005, EWS was looking to dispense with its Class 37 fleet and so Arriva Trains Wales hired in Riviera Trains (RT) '4/s' to cover the diagrams in question. Thus, RT's No 47839, in Oxford blue, can be seen accelerating up the hill, over Pontlottyn Viaduct on the final leg of the 2R38 16.50 Cardiff Central-Rhymney on Friday 12 August 2005.

After many false finishes, the last locomotive-hauled train along this route finally came when No 37410 formed the 2F10 07.47 Rhymney to Cardiff on Monday 11 December 2006. *Adrian Kenny*

Fowey in Cornwall is generally known for its quaint, narrow twisting streets and its bustling harbour. Not noticed by the casual visitor is its role as Britain's largest china clay port, the clay being brought in daily from the local driers by rail. With the clay hood wagons and hydraulic locomotives long gone, the last years of the 20th century will be remembered for the small fleet of dedicated '37/5' and the white CDA clay hoppers that plied up and down the four-mile Lostwithiel to Fowey branch, taking their loads to the harbour for export far and wide.

Arriving at Carne Point, the railway name for Fowey, No 37670 waits with 6P00 09.10 from Drinnick Mill on a glorious 18 May 1998; the locomotive, the former No 37182 had originally been allocated to Laira for clay traffic way back in 1982, and although it strayed a few times, it remained a Cornish engine until displaced by the Class 66 invasion in 1999. After dropping its wagons, it would soon return with a set of empties to Lostwithiel, where, after running round, it would head west again for reloading at a location on that day's train plan. *Neil Higson*

By 28 May 2003, a period of almost 20 years had slipped by since the closure of Coulsdon North. The site where Coulsdon North signalbox once proudly stood, between the Quarry line and the route via Redhill had returned to nature's tenure. As one of only a handful of electro-diesels to receive EWS colours, No 73131 sped past leading the 1090 16.30 Willesden Railnet to Dover. This was one of the final railborne postal services and was made up of Royal Mail and Rail Express Systems-liveried stock, with No 73136 'tailing'. Rail Express Systems, or RES, was formed in October 1991 to streamline the Parcels Sector, the smallest of the British Rail sectors, the others being InterCity, Network SouthEast, Provincial and Railfreight. No 73131 began life as E6038. *Mark Darby*

No 37429 *Eisteddfod Genedlaethol* heads 1D69, the 12.18 Crewe to Holyhead Regional Railways service with a matching rake of four coaches. The train is crossing Pen-y-Clip Viaduct after emerging from the short tunnel of the same name. These tunnels are a feature of the North Wales coast as the railway hugs the cliffs and coastline.

The photograph taken on 20 July 1996 was only possible for a short period in summer months as shadows from the cliffs and A55 dual carriageway from where the photo was taken cover the foreground for most of the year.

In the distance behind Conwy Bay can be seen the Great Ormes Head. Many visits were made to North Wales at this time as locomotive-hauled services were to finish for good, but as with all things railway, they change and since then Class 47s and 57s have regularly worked Manchester to Holyhead trains. In 2007, Class 57/3s were dragging Class 390 Pendolinos on daily services between Holyhead and Crewe whilst Class 67s were crew training for Arriva Trains Wales. *Paul Higgins*

The advent of competition on the railways meant that in 2006 and 2007, there were five different freight trains on the Perth to Aberdeen line, whereas pre-privatisation, there would have been perhaps two. EWS was operating two trains, one for parcels and one for 'Enterprise' traffic; Freightliner Heavy Haul was operating a weekly cement train, DRS a daily intermodal service and GBRf an 'as required' load of 'mud oil'. This was great for photography, but was it great for the railway as a whole?

The DHL parcels traffic operated by EWS tended to be loaded one way only, that being to Aberdeen. However, from April 2005, the 5D03 Aberdeen to Mossend empties were replaced by a 1M07 18.10 Aberdeen to Walsall loaded service. It is with this train that No 67011 is seen in glorious conditions having just passed over Muchall Mills Viaduct on Thursday 5 May 2005. Unfortunately, this working lasted only four months and 1M07 soon reverted to its previous 5D03 slot. Worse was to follow, as in early 2007, the DHL parcels traffic to both Aberdeen and Inverness was lost to road haulage altogether. *Adrian Kenny*

No 56046 built at Doncaster in 1978 had an uneventful career until early 1993, when it was one of six Class 56s rendered surplus by Trainload Freight and taken over by Network SouthEast for civil engineering duties, each locomotive supposedly replacing a pair of 33s. All received a G exam overhaul at Doncaster and repaint into the new civil engineers 'Dutch' livery of grey and yellow. Under the changes that occurred prior to British Rail being split up and sold, the '56s' soon ended up back on their old Trainload Freight duties!

On the first day of May 2002 the class still had a stronghold on the Boulby branch in the northeast, where No 56046 rounds one of the many curves on the Middlesborough-Boulby Mine branch at North Skelton, working the 6F38 17.00 Boulby-Tees Dock. The JGA and JIA hopper wagons, loaded at Cleveland Potash with rock salt, are then unloaded at the discharge facility at Tees Dock. Soon after this photograph, the '56s' were replaced by EWS Class 66s, and although the trains still run on this scenic line, they are now in the hands of Freightliner Heavy Haul '66s'. *Neil Higson*

Four fruitless round trips of around 150 miles each were undertaken specifically to capture the 'purple monster' as it was dubbed by enthusiasts, in action on the Berks & Hants line, and despite frequently inaccurate weather forecasts this view was eventually secured. On 17 July 2002, No 57601, the former No 47825 *Thomas Telford*, would have been using its 2,500hp two-stroke General Motors 'transplant' to good effect as it galloped through Wootton Rivers with a smart rake of First Great Western liveried Mk 2 'aircons', forming the morning's 1C34 07.30 Plymouth to London Paddington. The Kennet & Avon canal, long associated with the Berks &

Hants, trails in behind the trees at this location, running parallel to the line almost all the way to Reading. This particular locomotive was numbered D1759 when delivered new, becoming No 47165 prior to ETH conversion as No 47590. After re-classification to a '47/8' a number of years passed before it was chosen to become Porterbrook's 'Thunderbird' demonstrator, when a major rebuild introduced an almost brand new locomotive, unveiled to the world on 26 March 2001 in an imposing silver and purple livery. *Mark Darby*

Possibly the best of the pre-privatisation liveries was Loadhaul's black and orange colours and these are shown to good effect in this 27 October 1994 shot. No 37713 powers four TTA fuel tanks running as the 6G85 10.54 Lindsey Oil Refinery to Neville Hill Depot and passes the lime dust-covered Singleton Birch lime factory at Melton Ross on Humberside. On arrival the fuel would have been used in the HST and units using the large Leeds depot at the time.

This working is an unusual one on the very busy freight artery between the Humberside refineries to the east and their various destinations in the west, as most trains were, and still are, lengthy block services. The line between Immingham and the semaphore-signalled Barnetby is still popular today, being one of the country's busiest places to photograph freight trains carrying iron ore, coal and oil and much else. *Paul Higgins*

The privatisation of the network has led to several entrepreneurs in the industry carving out a niche for themselves in this complicated market. Although firms like Ian Riley and Pete Waterman have withdrawn from the mainline and other firms such as Fragonset have gone into receivership, several other companies such as Riviera Trains and the West Coast Railway Company have made a success of their venture and are now firmly established.

This also applies to Cotswold Rail, which from humble beginnings has branched out from Anglia 'Thunderbird' duties by acquiring further locomotives (mainly, but not all, Class 47s) a freight operator's licence (Advenza), coaching stock (the 'Blue Pullman' set) and despite having its own charter arm marketed under the Heartland Rail banner, also the Steamy Affairs railtour operator in 2007.

Cotswold Rail's silver livery is now a well recognised brand and is seen here on No 47828 *Joe Strummer* and No 47813 *John Peel* which are towing five rather mixed coaches on a Santa Special Mystery tour. Fortunately for the photographers, it wasn't *that* much of a mystery and the 1Z47 10.29 Gloucester to Gloucester via Bath, the Berks & Hants, Reading West Curve, Swindon, Westbury (run round) and Bath (again) is seen passing Newton St Loe west of Bath Spa on Saturday 16 December 2006. *Adrian Kenny*

With snow-capped Moeldda in the background, Arriva turquoise No 158840 crosses the Dwyryd River at Penrhyndeudraeth, three miles south of Porthmadog, whilst working the 08.00 Pwllheli–Machynlleth service on 10 April 2006. Production of the Class 158 totalled 182 units, 155840 being the last 'standard' two-car unit fitted with a 350hp Cummins engine, others being either with a 350hp Perkins or 400hp Cummins unit.

The train has just passed the location of Cook's explosives factory, which at its peak during World War II employed more than 600 people. The company made extensive use of rail for distribution, but when the sidings were closed in the late 1970s following the withdrawal of freight traffic from the Cambrian route, a new facility was constructed at Maentwrog Road on the Blaenau Ffestiniog-Trawsfynydd section of the Conwy Valley line. By 1997, after 75 years of production, Cook's had closed, and the site cleared, to make way for a nature reserve.
*Neil Higson*

Arguably the most famous of all railway engineers, the name *Isambard Kingdom Brunel* has graced the flanks of several fine locomotives over the years, including No 5069, one of Charles Collett's beautiful 'Castle' class, and also Brush Type 4 No 47484. The latest incumbent, No 60081, was outshopped in a lined green livery and named at the Old Oak Common open weekend in August 2000. Interrupting only the whistling of wading birds *'IKB'* skirts the River Severn at Purton on 10 August 2001 hauling 6B13, the 05.36 Robeston to Westerleigh Murco oil terminal. No 60081's career came to a premature end after a crankcase explosion caused a severe engine-room fire on 3 April 2005, whilst leading the 6L55 10.15 Llandudno Junction to Crewe Basford Hall Yard, through Beeston Castle. At the time of writing (mid-2007) No 60081 was still supporting the cast name and numberplates, albeit dumped at Toton Depot. *Mark Darby*

Milford Junction in Yorkshire is a popular location for railway enthusiasts and photographers alike, as seen in this view of National Power-operated No 59202 *Vale of White Horse* hauling a rake of matching coal hoppers. The train is about one mile into its journey to Drax power station, from the now closed Gascoigne Wood 'super pit' on 18 July 1996.

National Power was one of the original post-BR private railway operators, using its own fleet of six Class 59/2 locomotives which were shedded at Ferrybridge.

In 1997 National Power decided to offload its rail operation, with EWS gaining the work from 1998. The '59/2s' gained EWS house colours and continued to work around their old haunts as well as spreading their wings to Peak Forest. They were then transferred *en masse* to Hither Green for stone trains out of Acton, but are presently concentrated on Westbury where their haulage capacity can be put to best use. *Paul Higgins*

The Avonmouth Enterprise traffic has varied considerably over the years, from domestic coal to containers, from fertiliser to foodstuffs and from mineral water to soap powder. Currently the main traffic is paper from Scandinavia, imported via Tilbury.

Following EWS's loss of the Travelling Post Office and other mail traffic, its fleet of 30 'Skips' (Class 67s) became practically redundant. However, new uses as 'Thunderbirds', powering test trains, new parcels traffic, additional charter trains and most unexpectedly, light freight duties, have been found for the class.

EWS unveiled its Managers Train on the 19 October 2004 at Toton, formed of three coaches, DVT 82146 and 67029, which had been specially modified to be compatible with the DVT. Surprisingly perhaps, EWS colours were not adopted for the train, the company instead opting for a striking silver colour for the '67' and DVT, and a deep lined maroon for the coaches.

Combining all of the above three elements, we find that on St David's Day 2007, No 67029 has 10 empty IZA twin Cargowaggons in tow, forming the 6M33 16.23 Avonmouth CT to Wembley Yard. The train is pictured at Hallen Moor, soon after the start of its journey. *Adrian Kenny*

No 37519, still in obsolete Trainload Metals livery, thrashes away from Frome with the summer-dated 2086 08.30 Bristol Temple Meads-Weymouth on Tuesday 14 July 1999. 2O86 was usually a '37/4' turn, resulting in every one, except 37410, of the ETH sub-class completing a return trip to the coast. By November No 37519 had been withdrawn due to excessive engine fumes, and despite its low engine hours was doomed never to run again. It was stored for many years at Eastleigh before being sold to CF Booth, Rotherham for scrap in November 2007.

In the early 1980s it became a minor celebrity engine when as 37027 it was transferred from its original base of East Anglia to Scotland, to help in the displacement of Class 27s on the West Highland lines. On arrival it was painted with the wrap around yellow painted cabs and in the BR blue era this was indeed a welcome move. *Neil Higson*

If only Briton Ferry was this busy on a regular daily basis. The 2001 Football Association Cup Final at the Millennium Stadium was responsible for this hectic scene. On 12 May three rakes of empty stock were on view. No 67014 with an almost complete rake of Anglia turquoise-liveried vehicles, the uniformity interrupted only by a solitary InterCity Mk 2 left first, to form 1Z91, the 18.00 Cardiff Central to Finsbury Park. Back in the yard, No 67018 waited with another rake of Anglia-liveried coaches (which at the time were being loaded with much commiserative beer!)

to form 5Z95 ECS to Cardiff, working onward as 1Z95 the 19.00 to Finsbury Park. Completing the scene, was RES-liveried No 47780 with the Northern Belle stock, prior to working back as 1Z81, the 18.55 Cardiff Central to London Euston. The Arsenal fans heading back to the capital would certainly not have toasted Liverpool's Michael Owen, his two late goals securing a 2-1 win for the Merseysiders. *Mark Darby*

In the 1980s, when these two locomotives were introduced, the disillusioned steam photographers of the day would probably have packed their cameras away in disgust at either English Electric Type 3, No D6744, or Brush Type 4 No D1666 (which later became *Odin*). Some 40 years later, on Saturday 19 October 2002, attitudes have changed, as the photographer was 'very impressed' to record No 37710 in Loadhaul colours, leading RES-liveried No 47778

*Irresistible* making a fine sight heading the 4M03 09.21 Brighton Lovers Walk to Derby. Consisting of EWS 'translator' vans, the double-heading of four vehicles was a result of two previous overnight deliveries of new electric units to the former Southern Region. Running on the bi-directional slow line, the ensemble approaches Wellingborough. Colourful combinations such as this are one of the positive aspects of the post-privatisation railway scene. *Paul Higgins*

At 261ft long, Bridge No 137 on the Settle & Carlisle line is better known by a far more romantic name. On 31 July 2004, crew and passengers alike have just enjoyed the scenic delights of Mallerstang, as No 37411 *The Scottish Railway Preservation Society* negotiates Ais Gill Viaduct, whilst crossing Ais Gill Beck leading the customary rake of four Arriva Mk 2 air-conditioned coaches forming 1E23 the 15.32 Carlisle to Leeds. On this outing No 37411's usual partner No 37408 *Loch Rannoch* was 'tailing' the formation. After a couple of weeks' crew training Arriva Trains North re-introduced locomotive-hauled passenger stock onto the S&C on 13 October 2003. The English Electric 12 CSVT powered partners pictured here were originally consecutively numbered D6989 (37408 ex-37289) and D6990, the latter becoming No 37290 before being No 37411. *Mark Darby*

The 'Royal Scotsman' is a well-known and popular train to photograph in Scotland since it first started to operate in 1985. Even though it is nine coaches long, the number of passengers – or guests as they are referred to – is a maximum of 36 at any one time. From April to October 2004, trains were operating to a two-day long 'Wee Dram', three-day 'Highland', four-day 'Western' or five-day 'Classic' fixed itinerary, which between them, covered all of the major lines in Scotland except the Far North.

This view at Carmont, shows the Royal Scotsman coaches to good effect behind No 37421,

whilst working the 1H90 14.30 Edinburgh to Keith on Tuesday 15 June 2004. This is the first leg of the five-day 'Classic' tour, going to Kyle via Aberdeen and returning to Edinburgh via Aviemore. EWS had, over the years, painted variously Nos 37428, 37401 and 37416 in the Royal Scotsman livery as dedicated locomotives to operate the train. No 37428 had been withdrawn in December of the previous year, and one presumes none of the other two dedicated locomotives were available on this occasion. *Adrian Kenny*

On a hot 28 June 2003 the VSOE with No 47767 *Saint Columba* running as 1Z27 the 14.18 Haverfordwest to Cardiff makes a rare visit to West Wales, and is shown passing the Afon Tywi, St Ishmael, near Carmarthen.

No 47767, formerly D1672 was new to Cardiff Canton on 27 March 1965. By August of that year it was one of 18 Western Region '47s' to be named after Greek Gods, *Colossus* being its chosen name, which was removed sometime in the mid 1980s. Staying on the Western for many years it became No 47086 and then, in 1986, after ETH fitting, No 47641, and finally in the EWS era, No 47767. It was one of the Class 47s involved in the EWS reliability programme in 2003, and after release in full EWS colours, complete with snow ploughs was put to use mainly on Charters. Unfortunately the locomotive caught fire near Hook on 4 July 2003 when on a Victoria-Southampton VSOE, and this spelt the end for this fine locomotive. It also spelt the end for Class 47s on such workings, as VSOE requested only '67s' after this date. *Neil Higson*

In 1998, the final full year of EWS 'Crompton' operation, aggregates traffic in conjunction with construction of Croydon Tramlink was one of the best bets to produce Class 33 haulage. Monday 14 September, however, was a disappointment to the gathered photographers as Transrail-branded No 60082 *Mam Tor* approached Earleswood with a rake of eight empty Brett high capacity hoppers forming an additional 6Y94 09.36 MWX Purley to Cliffe via Salfords working. Transrail, livery-wise, was the least imaginative of the pre-privatised British Rail freight companies formed in 1994 (the others were Mainline and Loadhaul). Its purpose was to operate freight services in South West England, Wales, the North West of England and Scotland. Mam Tor, an Iron Age fort overlooking Castleton and the beautiful Hope Valley, was a name accurately matched to part of No 60082's allocated sphere of operation. *Mark Darby*

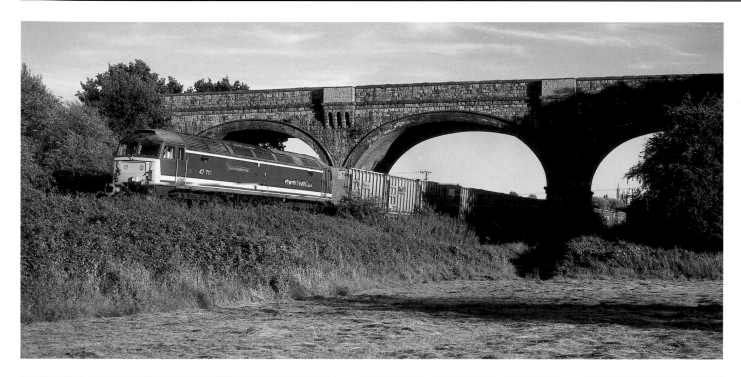

In 1998 the Avon 'bin train' was justifiably famous for using locomotives from Immingham's LWCW Infrastructure pool, which consisted of a motley collection of '47s' in a variety of heritage liveries. The train served three terminals at Westmoreland in Bath, Barrow Road in Bristol and Westerleigh, where each wagon of three containers would be lifted off and replaced with a full container of domestic waste.

No 47711 *County of Hertfordshire* has eight fully loaded KFAs in tow ambling up the Westerleigh branch with 4C06 the 20.00 Westerleigh-Stoke Gifford on Friday 7 August 1998. The last EWS-hauled Avon Bin train ran with No 66040 on Friday 30 March 2001 and Freightliner took over the following Monday.

Freightliner has operated to a simpler itinerary and schedule than EWS by concentrating on the Bath and Bristol terminals and missing out the Westerleigh portion altogether. Although the wagons are currently the same as before, Avon County Council procured new boxes, making this shot of No 47711, its containers and location a part of history three times over. *Adrian Kenny*

No 37197 hauling the 1Z48 Carlisle to Newcastle 'Green Express' charter made a pleasant surprise storming south at Armathwaite on 31 August 2004, as the locomotive was supposed to be on the rear, not No 47854 as depicted! The 12 immaculate West Coast Railway Company Maroon Mk 2s will make the engine work hard as it heads south along the Settle & Carlisle line, to the enjoyment of the '37' fans no doubt in the front coach.

The 1964-built two tone green engine was one of the early privately owned and operated locomotives, being resurrected by Bury-based, Ian Riley Engineering, after EWS had deemed it surplus in 1999. When Ian Riley pulled out of the main line diesel scene it was bought by DRS and is currently stored waiting repairs, de-registered at Carlisle Kingmoor. *Paul Higgins*

A most popular gesture by Virgin Trains was the repainting of No 86233 into original 'electric blue' livery. The former *Laurence Olivier* gained a cast lion and wheel emblem, raised numberplates, including re-application of original pre-TOPS number E3172 along with *Alsthom Heritage* nameplates. Presentation to the press came at Willesden Traincare Depot on 24 June 2002, and was to symbolise Alstom's heritage within the UK rail industry. On the evening of

12 July 2003 E3172 heads for Northampton at Milton Malsor with a rake of mainly Mk 2s and DVT forming the diverted 16.50 London Euston to Wolverhampton service. The Class 86s, or 'AL6s' as they were originally termed, covered many millions of miles during their illustrious careers, and although more common than their Class 87 cousins, they were arguably more charismatic. *Mark Darby*

A photograph of five different liveries on one train made this a must for inclusion in the book. Taking a rare main line outing on 4 October 1999, Peak No D172 (46035) hauls the 7Z41 09.10 Bishops Lydeard to Kidderminster working. The convoy included No 50149 in Railfreight General livery, Class 42 'Warship', No D832 *Onslaught* in BR blue, Class 24 No D5054 (24054) in black and Class 40 D345 (40145) in BR green. The locomotives had been used on the West Somerset Railway for a diesel gala and were moving onto the next event *en bloc*! The headboard 'Auntie Jayne's Therapeutic Outing' remains a mystery. Answers on a postcard please!

In the background can be seen Barton Hill depot still in its heyday, with no fewer than five Class 47s awaiting their next turn of duty.

This is the only picture in the book not using Fuji film, Kodak Ektachrome E200 being given a one-off trial at the time. *Neil Higson*

During the autumn of 1998 Silverlink was suffering poor availability of its DMU fleet on the Bletchley to Bedford route. The answer was a trial period of one week utilising Nos 31468 and 31452 from Fragonset Railways and two Forward Trust Mk 2a coaches, TSO *Michaela* and BSO *Ellen*. In this photograph, No 31468 makes a spirited departure from the Woburn Sands station stop, whilst working the 10.50 Bletchley to Bedford service on 12 October 1998. The line today has changed totally; the signalbox and semaphore signals have all gone, being replaced with colour light signals controlled from a new signalling centre at Ridgemont.

The trial was a success with locomotive and coaches starting on regular service trains from March 1999. Today the line is operated by Class 150 Sprinter units. *Paul Higgins*

With the highly unusual prospect of a locomotive-hauled train returning to the Exeter to Waterloo line, west of Salisbury, the Ordnance Survey map was duly consulted and checked against the timings. The weather forecast was good, so a spot a few miles west of Yeovil Junction was selected, however 13 years had elapsed since a visit had last been made to photograph No 50046 *Ajax* ... would the location still be clear? On 30 March 2004 the view was as vegetation-free as it was back in 1991. Running to time, split headcode box fitted No 37042 stormed through Stoford with a rake of Serco and Railtrack branded stock forming 1Z14, the 07.43 Bournemouth Traction Depot to Salisbury East Yard via Exeter St Davids. No 37109 'tailed' the formation. Former numbers of the locomotives were D6742 and D6809 respectively.
*Mark Darby*

Apart from a few single-car 'Bubbles', heritage DMUs finally bowed out from the national network on 24 December 2003 when sets 101678 and 101685 worked the 2H59 21.10 Rose Hill-Manchester Piccadilly. In the last few years the remaining Metropolitan Cammell Class 101s, once a fleet of 760 cars, saw out their days on services around South Manchester, with Marple and Rose Hill Marple services being favoured by the planners. On 6 January 2004 the last five units were towed to Pigs Bay, Shoeburyness for storage. Most have been sold on to preservationists.

On 16 March 2003 No 101676, a power-twin consisting of cars 51205, 51803 approaches Romiley with the 11.14 Manchester Piccadilly-Rose Hill Marple service in Regional Railways colours. Both the vehicles are now preserved, leading car No 51205 in BR green at the Cambrian Railways Trust near Oswestry, Shropshire and 1958-built No 51803 at the Keighley & Worth Valley Railway. *Neil Higson*

One of the more unusual services in recent times has been the working of an additional train to Aberystwyth in July or August for a two-week long Jewish convention held in the town. This is then followed by a similar return trip to take the delegates back again. The train has only run twice with locomotive haulage, as units have been found to run the train in other years. The service has not been operated as a charter, but as an additional working, enabling 'bashers' to sample the delights of Class 37 haulage over a line long without a locomotive-hauled service of any kind

The first locomotive-hauled train ran on 22 July 2002 with No 37421 (returning with the same locomotive on 5 August), whilst the second train ran on Wednesday 17 August 2005 behind No 37427 *Bont Y Bermo*, also returning with the same locomotive, on 31 August. The outward leg of the 2005 train ran as a 1Z37 14.51 Birmingham New Street to Aberystwyth and is pictured here framed amongst the trees and semaphores at Cosford between Wolverhampton and Shrewsbury. *Adrian Kenny*

On the outskirts of Britain's densely populated second city of Birmingham in the West Midlands, Nos 31407 and 31110 storm out of Walsall at Ryecroft Junction with 7F63, the 08.38 Bescot Yard to Stud Farm empty ballast train heading onto the Sutton Park line, on 2 June 1997. Its consist of short-wheelbase ZFV Dogfish ballast wagons was typical of the time. Today, vacuum braked four-wheel ballast hoppers, along with the pairs of Class 31s hauling them, are history, as engineers' trains today use high capacity bogie hoppers in fixed sets, with Class 66 locomotives the preferred option to move them, due to their slow speed capabilities, which are useful when unloading.

No 31407 was the only Class 31 to receive Mainline blue livery and if not immaculate, it is certainly a lot cleaner than the yellow and dark grey 'Dutch' livery of veteran No 31110 which is not even as clean as its wagons. Waiting in the background at the signal to continue towards Bescot is No 47293 in RfD colours. *Paul Higgins*

Privatisation at its absolute best! With its Napier Deltic power plant reverberating through the early morning Northamptonshire air, D9000 *Royal Scots Grey* leaves Weedon behind as it approaches Stowe Hill Tunnel with 1O99, the 06.58 Birmingham New Street to Ramsgate summer Saturday dated service on 18 June 1999. The Class 55 was diagrammed throughout, and booked to return with the 1S87 12.10 Ramsgate to Glasgow Central via the Western Region main line and Oxford, with electric traction taking over at Birmingham New Street.

Placed onto the books of British Railways on 28 February 1961, D9000 had to wait until 18 June the following year to be named. Renumbering to 55022 came in April 1974. The axe fell with premature withdrawal on 2 January 1982. That was until private operation beckoned …
*Mark Darby*

No 73101 The *Royal Alex* is shown arriving at Southampton East Dock QE II terminal with the VSOE boat train from London Victoria on 3 September 1999, so passengers could join the famous Cunard liner of the same name. The locomotive was painted into the Pullman livery for a 21 September 1991 special working of the 'Brighton Belle' utilising the VSOE stock, from Victoria to Brighton, to commemorate 150 years of the London-Brighton route. It was named after the famous Royal Alexandra Children's Hospital, near to the station, by Michael Bulleid, grandson of the famous Southern Railway engineer.

Built as E6007 and despatched from English Electric's Vulcan Works, Newton-le-Willows, as the first 'JB' electro-diesel on 13 October 1967, the locomotive was renumbered 73101 in 1980 and named *Brighton Evening Argus*, to celebrate the paper's centenary that year. Twenty-two years later in May 2002, this 1600hp 750V dc, and 600hp diesel, locomotive was finally withdrawn from Hither Green. EWS disposed of it to Booth Roe Metals at Rotherham, but it quickly found itself preserved by the Dean Forest Diesel Association, initially at Lydney, and is currently on loan to the Severn Valley Railway. *Neil Higson*

Passing the site of Bagworth station on the Knighton South Junction-Burton on Trent route in Leicestershire, Nos 37707 and 37375 power 6Z77, the 12.05 Stud Farm to Crewe Basford Hall Yard on 20 October 2003. A former coal stronghold, the area now only has two quarries generating rail traffic, the other apart from Stud Farm, being Bardon Hill. The train will continue to the southern end of the freight-only line and join the Midland main line for a short distance before taking the route to Nuneaton and then heading north up the West Coast main line (WCML) to its destination. The train is made up of former BSC iron ore tippler wagons displaced from the South Wales iron ore circuit and designated JUAs.

This bulk ballast service will be unloaded at the virtual quarry at Crewe, from where the stone will be reloaded into other specialist wagons required for dedicated engineering trains. Although this double-handles the stone, it saves all the smaller wagons having to go to the quarry each time for loading. *Paul Higgins*

No 60040 hauling former National Power JMA coal hoppers (NP 19600 -19650) now used for limestone, passes the storage sheds at Great Rocks with 6H37, the 07.32 Bredbury to Tunstead. The Tilcon terminal at Bredbury, near Stockport receives up to two trains a day from Tunstead, which is one of Europe's super quarries producing more than 5.5 million tonnes of limestone annually. With a large proportion despatched by rail, the area has become a stronghold for the 3100hp Class 60s due to their haulage capacity being well suited to the heavy trains. No 60040, the former *Brecon Beacons* entered traffic for Trainload Construction on 6 February 1992, being one of a small batch allocated to Stewarts Lane FASB pool for use in the southeast.

Although appearing as double-track, this section of the former Midland Railway is in fact a single line to Buxton, paralleled by the entrance to Tunstead, this being the route No 60040 is taking.
*Neil Higson*

**Opposite:** With the tranquil waters of Afon Conwy providing a pleasant foreground, Regional Railways-liveried No 37429 *Eisteddfod Genedlaethol* curves away from the majestic Conwy Castle, hauling 1K58, the 07.37 Holyhead to Crewe service; photographed on 31 May 1997. Regional Railways reintroduced locomotive-hauled stock onto the scenic North Wales coast line in 1993. This lasted officially until the end of 2000; however; the final locomotive and coaches formation ran on 20 January 2001, the last rites being undertaken by No 37429 sporting a commemorative headboard. From April 1986, prior to being named *Eisteddfod Genedlaethol* the following August, 37429 carried the name *Sir Dyfed – County of Dyfed*. Previous numbers were D6600 and 37300. *Mark Darby*

There is no argument in the road-versus-rail contest when one considers how many HGVs this train would be keeping off our heavily congested roads. A single GBRf Class 66 locomotive, No 66708 effortlessly lifts its well-loaded container train up Belstead bank, just south of Ipswich, on 30 October 2007. The train has just passed over the busy A14 trunk route that provides the competition. The photograph shows the diverted 4E33 11.04 Felixstowe to Doncaster railport

Medite service, which is going via London instead of its booked route via Ely. The diversion is necessary due to the rebuilding of the bridge spanning the River Ouse at Ely, after the serious damage caused by the derailment of the 6L58 Mountsorrel to Chelmsford on 22 June 2007.

The General Motors invaders from across the Atlantic are not everyone's favourite; however, after nine years in service they are here to stay. *Paul Higgins*

The Cambrian line saw something of a locomotive-hauled revival in 2005 with a variety of services run as both railtours and engineering trains. Even though Class 66s were eventually cleared as far as Tywyn, the restricted route availability of the line meant that '37s' were the preferred choice of traction on railtours – for more than one obvious reason!

Here, 37406 *The Saltire Society* is seen at the head of Past Time Rail's 'Cambrian Coast Flyer' approaching Friog Cliffs to the south of Barmouth. The train is diagrammed as 1Z38, the 16.30 Pwllheli to Bristol Temple Meads and the date is Saturday 16 July 2005. *Adrian Kenny*

No 47712 *Artemis* in Nanking Blue with the matching Blue Pullman train, passes Arn Hill near Warminster with 1Z53, the 1727 Salisbury-Victoria on 06.06.06! This superb train was launched by FM Rail on 5 January 2006, with a short circular tour from Derby to Manchester and return for the lucky guests. The luxury dining train proved to be very popular, and was kept busy with a full programme of tours. Marketed under the Hertfordshire Tours arm of FM Rail, it came to a sudden halt when FM Rail went into receivership in 2006.

Artemis is the Greek goddess of wilderness, hunting and childbirth and the locomotive is a

Brush Falcon Works product, entering service as D1948 on 1 August 1966. After a spell as No 47505 it was selected for conversion into a Class 47/7 for use on the Edinburgh-Glasgow push-pull services of the early 1980s, being named *Lady Diana Spencer* on 30 April 1981 at Glasgow Queen Street. By April 1995 it was Waterman Railways' *Dick Whittington* before finally becoming *Artemis* in January 2001. After the FM Rail collapse it was stored at Derby after being purchased by DRS for possible further use. *Neil Higson*

The pioneer Class 37, the former D6700 and 37119 was, when photographed on 27 April 1999, sporting former British Railways green livery, lion & wheel emblem, numbered 37350 and carrying the ornate nameplate *National Railway Museum*. It was recorded near Penybedd between Kidwelly and Pembrey with 6Z93, the 15.15 WO Carmarthen to Newport Alexandra Dock Junction. This train was composed of empty Cargowaggons which had previously arrived in West Wales loaded with fertilizer that had originated from Norsk Hydro, at Immingham, and only recently returned to rail. This particular location was a little over a quarter of a mile from the former Burry Port & Gwendraeth Valley branch, which paralleled the main line at this point. The BP&GV was synonymous with Class 03s and 08s which due to loading gauge restrictions had cut-down cabs, so that they could work to the washery at Coedbach until its closure in 1998.
*Mark Darby*

Back in 2002 there was an endless procession of locomotive-hauled trains along the WCML, hauled by Class 87s and a full supporting cast of Class 86s and 90s. Most trains at the time were hauled by Virgin liveried machines, however hired-in traction was also used as required from Freightliner or, as shown here, EWS. On 10 June of that year, at Brockhall, Northamptonshire, EWS-liveried No 86261 The *Rail Charter Partnership* sweeps past with a service bound for Scotland.

This particular English Electric-built 'AL6' started life as E3118 in 1965. TOPS saw the application of 86041 and upon receipt of flexicoil suspension and SAB resilient wheels, the locomotive became a member of the '86/2' sub-class. SAB (the Swedish manufacturer, part of the SAB-Wabco group) wheels had rubber cushioning within the wheel itself, to alleviate bogie frame fractures and track damage caused by the weight of the unsprung, axle hung traction motors, when running at high speed. *Paul Higgins*

**Opposite:** No 37417 *Richard Trevithick* and numerical neighbour 37416 have 11 maroon-liveried coaches in tow, heading a return Scottish Railway Preservation Society/North East Railtours charter from Oban to Newcastle as the 1Z38 16.00 departure from the Scottish port. The train is on the approach to Lower Tyndrum on Bank Holiday Monday 2 May 2005. *Adrian Kenny*

Growling slowly up the Ebbw Valley in South Wales Nos 37886 and 37707 power the 1Z42 07.04 from Crewe, 'Onllwyn Orbiter' on 2 June 2001. Having just passed through the small town of Cwm, two miles short of Ebbw Vale, this Pathfinder tour had also visited Barry, Tondu and Margam Yard, but due to the condition of the track to Onllwyn, the train never got to its intended destination!

The line from Park Junction to Ebbw Vale was still busy at the time with three or four daily trains of steel coil for the tinplate works. The works shut on 5 July 2002 and shortly afterwards the line was taken out of use, but in 2008 it is planned to be open again, as a passenger line, a use this line has not seen since 30 April 1962!

Anyone intending to visit this location at Cwm will be in for a shock as a new road, the Cwm bypass, now runs parallel with the railway at this point; the rural nature of the shot is now sadly lost. *Neil Higson*

Having secured the aggregate industries' contract from the grasp of English Welsh & Scottish, which had commenced on 1 April 2006, Freightliner management moved swiftly to cover motive power shortages by hiring in two Direct Rail Services locomotives. No 66407 arrived at the beginning of the month, followed a few days later by No 66409. On Good Friday (14 April 2006)

DRS Compass-branded No 66409 is seen powering through Catholme, past Central Rivers traction depot, with a rake of loaded Freightliner Heavy Haul HHA hoppers forming 6M51, the 12.37 Hull King George Dock-Rugeley power station. The coal had been imported from Poland. *Mark Darby*

An early start was required to secure this photograph of No 47818 on its first passenger working in ONE Railway livery, hauling No 90003 *Raedwald of East Anglia* on a diverted 1G09 06.30 Norwich to London Liverpool Street service near Littlebury in Essex on 13 July 2004. The service was diesel-hauled and diverted due to the Ipswich Tunnel closure of 2004. The photograph highlights the livery changes that occur when franchises are gained and lost. The Class 47 engine is owned and hired from Cotswold Rail but carries ONE livery. The Class 90 is in the darker blue which initially appeared on these engines when ONE gained the Great Eastern franchise from the previous operator Anglia. The coaches are still painted in Anglia livery with a single InterCity coach.

The livery has received the nickname 'Refresher', after the sweet wrappers, due to the bright cab surrounds. Class 47 locomotives still work for ONE Railway on 'Thunderbird' duties and on summer Saturdays making regularly booked Norwich to Great Yarmouth drags with Class 90 locomotives and trains dead in tow. *Paul Higgins*

In a nice twist of fate, No 47828 *Severn Valley Railway – Kidderminster Bewdley Bridgnorth* is pictured only a very short distance from the subject of its nameplate. In the dying embers of the sun, the diverted 1V68 14.34 Newcastle to Bristol Temple Meads is captured crossing the 371yd Hoobrook Viaduct just over a mile south of Kidderminster on Sunday 29 April 2001. The locomotive had been named at the Severn Valley Railway's Kidderminster station only the day before this photograph was taken.

How times change though. No 47828 now carries the silver colours of its new owners, Cotswold Rail, and was named *Joe Strummer* at Bristol Temple Meads on 12 February 2005. *Adrian Kenny*

Class 205 '3H' unit No 205028 with its English Electric 4SRKT 600 HP engine, is seen thumping away from Crowborough, East Sussex forming the 16.04 Oxted-Uckfield shuttle on the evening of 12 August 2000. Crowborough, the sixth stop on this delightful branch line from Hurst Green, lies on the edge of the Ashdown Forest, home for many years to Sir Arthur Conan Doyle of Sherlock Holmes fame. The line became a branch on 4 May 1969 when the section beyond Uckfield to Lewes finally closed.

No 205028 was built at Eastleigh in 1962, numbered 1128, originally for the service between Salisbury and Reading and was designated a Berkshire unit. It was finally withdrawn in Connex yellow in December 2004, amazingly staying in its original formation for its 42 years of service. It is now preserved at Meldon on the Dartmoor Railway, arriving there on 3 January 2005 hauled by Nos 66708 and 73208. *Neil Higson*

Mainline branded 'Aircraft' blue and silver-liveried No 73136 *Kent Youth Music* potters along the non-electrified Marshlink route at Kingsnorth, on the southern outskirts of Ashford. It is hauling a solitary FNA, sandwiched between the customary barrier vehicles, forming 7062, the 06.29 Thursdays-only Willesden to Dungeness, on the morning of 13 August 1998. Dungeness Power Station, the destination of this working, is at the end of a short branch line from Appledore.

The electro-diesel would only be playing with the flask, even though it is operating on its 600hp English Electric 4-SRKT diesel engine. The nameplate 73136 is supporting relates to one of the largest music schools in Europe, which when named in May 1992 was situated well within traditional third rail territory at Maidstone, although the advent of Eurostar has brought 25kV also!
*Mark Darby*

Unofficially-named No 37415 'Mt Etna' and No 37419 pass Mobberley in Cheshire on 15 July 1996, powering the 7H55 11.05 ICI Oakleigh to Tunstead with the famed PHV vacuum braked limestone hopper wagons, some being 50 years old at this stage! In the past the trains would have been hauled by mainly by '8F' and '9F' steam engines, with Class 20s, 25s, 37s, 40s, 45s and 47s being just some of the locomotives used during the diesel era.

From January 1998 when the PHVs were finally withdrawn, Brunner Mond-branded JHA bogie stone hoppers hauled by a Class 60 have operated the service. Brunner Mond, which took over the ICI Tunstead works in 1993, continues to use thousands of tonnes of limestone each week as a raw material during the manufacture of soda ash, a raw ingredient used in the glassmaking industry.

During the 1990s various Tinsley '37/4s' gained unofficial hand-painted volcano names, chosen due to the locomotives' ability to discharge large amounts of smoke! *Paul Higgins*

No 37717 *Berwick Middle School Railsafe Trophy Winners 1998* and its load of 15 loaded OTA wagons powers past Helsby with the 6J33 19.02 Warrington-Chirk on 13 May 2003. The timber would have been loaded on the West Coast of Scotland with Taynuilt, Arrochar and Crianlarich being the preferred loading terminals at the time. On arrival at the Kronospan board mill at Chirk, the logs would have ended up as chipboard or MDF. In more recent times, EWS has lost this contract to Amec-Spie Rail (now Colas Rail) which, at the time of writing, uses hired-in Virgin West Coast Class 57/3s with IGA Ferry-Flat wagons.

Formerly No 37050, No 37717 was new to Sheffield Darnall shed after release from Vulcan Foundry on 24 August 1962, remaining an Eastern Region machine until 1988, apart from a short spell at Eastfield in early 1981. Named *Stainless Pioneer* in August 1992, a further three names were bestowed upon the locomotive over the years, all associated with the popular School Railsafe competitions of the late 1990s. *Neil Higson*

**Opposite:** No 57012 *Freightliner Envoy* has a long rake of wagons behind it whilst running past Caerleon with 4V08, the 18.30 Crewe Basford Hall to Wentloog. Normally this train would not be photographable in South Wales, but the combination of a long sunny summer evening on Monday 23 June 2003 and the train running just over an hour early, meant that by the time this photograph was taken at 20.11, there was still just about sufficient light to obtain an image.

Due to Wentloog moving from 24hr to 12hr operation, this service was discontinued and the last train ran on Friday 19 January 2007, leaving Freightliner with just one daily container service in the whole of Wales, to and from Southampton. *Adrian Kenny*

The unique Porterbrook purple and silver No 87002 carried alternative liveries either side. The curved colour scheme seen here, as opposed to the other, which carried a more angular silver panel running between cab doors with 'Porterbrook' emblazoned across it. Both designs incorporated the same colours. On 14 June 2003, it was caught for posterity propelling the diverted 13.35 Holyhead-London Euston away from Northampton, over the viaduct known locally as Fifteen Arches; spanning both the Grand Union Canal and the River Nene it carries the iron road towards the gloom of Hunsbury Hill Tunnel. The 'celebrity' electric would have taken over the baton from a Brush Type 4 at Crewe. *Mark Darby*

Where better to spend an hour on a balmy summer Saturday afternoon than in a field surrounded by buttercups overlooking the Settle & Carlisle line at Birkett Common? With over two dozen fellow photographers for company, a good 'social' was experienced prior to the main event.

Sole main line operational English Electric Class 40 'Whistler' No D345, looking splendid in early British Railways green livery, powers past the gathered gallery with a uniform rake of chocolate and cream Mk 1 coaching stock, forming 1Z41, a Carlisle to Bristol charter on 12 July 2003. All present went home very happy! *Paul Higgins*

One of the most colourful freight flows of recent years was the Freightliner Heavy Haul (FHH) block train of 15 blue Babcock 'Mega 3' intermodal wagons (KAA's) loaded with bright yellow Blue Circle branded cement lorry trailers.

The operation, funded by the Strategic Rail Authority enabled the trailers to be loaded at Westbury Cement works, and then after the 50-mile rail journey to Southampton Millbrook, lifted off the railway wagons so that they could be hauled by tractor units to the customer for unloading. Once empty they returned to Southampton for the journey back to Westbury.

The first loaded run was on 16 July 2003 hauled by No 47279, and it is seen approaching Warminster as the 6O77 07.38 Westbury Blue Circle-Southampton, with its impressive load. Unfortunately, after the initial contracted 50 trains, the operation was halted, and the wagons sent for long term store at Aberthaw cement works. As expected for the trailers, they are now a common sight on the roads around the southwest, their SRA logos still in place. No 47279, withdrawn as surplus by Freightliner by the end of 2003, was broken up by T J Thomson of Stockton in August 2007. *Neil Higson*

A classic example of a railway backwater; much of Lincolnshire retains anachronistic paraphernalia within its time-honoured infrastructure, as witnessed in this 2000 view of RES operated No 47734 *Crewe Diesel Depot – Quality Approved* hammering towards Saxilby at the head of a diverted GNER set, (with No 91010 dead at the rear) forming 1E03, the 10.00 Edinburgh Waverley to London Kings Cross. On the day of the photograph, 27 August, the East Coast main line (ECML) south of Doncaster was closed resulting in trains by-passing Lincoln by way of Pyewipe and Boultham Junctions before rejoining the normal route at Newark.

Taking to the rails as D1767 when new in October 1964, the locomotive had to wait until July 1979 to receive the name *County of Hertfordshire* during a ceremony at Hertford East whilst numbered 47172. The name was retained when reclassified in December 1981 into the '47/1' sub series as No 47583. As one of Stratford's favourites, it supported a special variation of the BR Large Logo livery in 1981 to honour the Royal wedding of Prince Charles and Lady Diana Spencer. Its 'county' nameplate was removed in June 1993, with the final name applied in March 1996. *Paul Higgins*

A popular train in the southwest is the 6V62 13.34 Fawley-Tavistock Junction (Plymouth) seen here on 10 August 2001 by No 66208 with its mixed load of bitumen and diesel fuel running alongside the River Exe at Powderham, with Exton and the Royal Marines Commando training centre at Lympstone on the opposite shore.

Railfreight Distribution started to run 6V62 in late January 1990, this block train taking over from previous Speedlink services that had carried the oil products from the huge Esso refinery at Fawley, near Southampton. In those days Class 47s were the norm, but with '33s', '37s', '50s', '58s' and '60s' used on odd occasions.

The bitumen is unloaded at the Esso facility at Cattewater, Plymouth, being tripped by Tavistock's Class 08 when required. As for the diesel fuel in the grey tanks, this is taken to Laira, St Blazey and Penzance on other EWS services. The empties will return with the same locomotive, normally within 30 minutes of the train's arrival at Tavistock, the Westbury crews being eager to get home! *Neil Higson*

Employees from the Mendip Quarries at Merehead and Whatley sampled twin Class 59 haulage on 17 October 1998. Liveried in Amey Roadstone's mustard yellow No 59101 *Village of Whatley* leads Foster Yeoman's No 59001 *Yeoman Endeavour* along the quadruple Western Region main line at Denchworth, with stock provided by Riviera Trains. At the civilised departure time of 09.08, this train, 1Z30, left Castle Cary, bound for Stratford-upon-Avon. No 47738 *Bristol Barton Hill* 'tailed' the formation. The RES Type 4 worked the return trip single-handedly, the Class 59s working light back to Merehead.

The Class 59, and therefore the subsequent builds of Class 66s can trace their roots back to 1983, when in the face of poor availability of British Rail locomotives, and the inability of any British locomotive manufacturer to build either new or existing types with the proven required reliability, Foster Yeoman looked to America and General Motors, whose products fitted the bill. From the signing of the contract in November 1984 to the unloading of Nos 59001-59004 at Southampton Docks on 22/23 January 1986, little over a year had elapsed; 14 months from conception to delivery was an amazing feat for a new design. A new era had begun. *Mark Darby*

The Royal Welsh Show is an annual occasion, held at Builth Wells, for all Welsh agricultural and livestock farmers to show off, buy, and sell their wares. Each year since 1998, with the exception of 2001, when the show was cancelled due to the foot and mouth epidemic, there have been locomotive-hauled specials to the four-day event. The weather for most years has not been the most conducive for colour photography and one had to be in the right place at the right time to get a result. Your photographer's first ever sunny photo of this event occurred at 19.23 on Wednesday 20 July 2005, when No 37425 and six coaches were captured crossing the Afon Sawdde, forming 1Z58, the 17.45 FSX Llandrindod Wells to Cardiff Central. *Adrian Kenny*

A service which now is nothing more than a memory was the affectionately known 'smelly' tanks, so nicknamed because of the unmistakeable lingering aroma of vinegar as the train passed by. This was acetic acid, which ironically is used, in part, in the manufacture of photographic film. The train was a true northeast-southwest cross-country freight, running from Humberside to South Wales.

On 5 August 1998, No 37803 resplendent in its Mainline Aircraft blue livery rushes through Croome Perry Wood, near Besford with a lengthy rake of short wheelbase tankers forming 6V14,

the 0835 Hull Saltend to Baglan Bay. The BP Chemicals Baglan Bay site was situated at the end of a short branch that ran from Briton Ferry Yard near Port Talbot. It has since closed and been demolished, resulting in yet another loss of traffic from the rail network.

One of a select band to operate infrastructure trains on SNCF metals over in France, No 37803, like the train it is illustrated hauling, is now defunct. Numbered D6908 when first delivered into capital stock, the number 37208 was also carried prior to conversion as a 'heavyweight' machine. *Paul Higgins*

Although Amec Spie Rail Systems Ltd had been operating on the rail network for a number of years, they first made the headlines on the 24 January 2007, when they took over the running of the timber trains from Carlisle (and later Arrochar & Tarbert), to Kronospan's timber factory at Chirk in North Wales. Amec plc later completed the disposal of its joint venture rail business with Spie to Colas SA in April 2007. At this time the timber trains were being hauled by 'hired in' Virgin 57/3s so Colas purchased two redundant EWS 47s and overhauled them at Eastleigh.

Colas had also won a contract with Network Rail to run the Devon- and Cornwall-based Rail Head Treatment Train (RHTT). Thus, on Sunday 21 October 2007, No 47727 *Rebecca* and No 47749 *Demelza* find themselves on Coldrennick Viaduct, emitting a plume of exhaust as they top and tail 3S11, the 11.54 Tavistock Junction Yard to Tavistock Junction Yard, via Newton Abbot and Liskeard. One has to note the irony of a company operating two contracts with locomotives bought from the company it also won the flows from! *Adrian Kenny*

On a beautiful clear summer morning No 59002 *Alan J. Day* heads west towards London, past the golden fields of Crofton in Wiltshire. On 6 August 2003 the uniquely-liveried Mendip Rail Class 59 heads the 7A09 07.05 Merehead to Acton Yard, 'jumbo' service made up of only Foster Yeoman bogie hoppers and EWS-owned OBA wagons at the rear, carrying concrete blocks for the building industry, both of which are unloaded at the terminal in Acton. This service can also carry a portion for Purfleet, but that was obviously not required on this day.

The locomotive's colour scheme was as a result of a joint venture between Foster Yeoman and ARC, to combine their own trains and rail operations, known as Mendip Rail. Today both companies have been taken over by bigger international construction companies and 59002 is back into Foster Yeoman's colours. *Paul Higgins*

There are many arguments over which is the better medium for photography – colour or black and white. This is one of the reasons 'for' colour photography. Although not necessarily complementary to each other, the yellow rape seed field, red HST and black sky in this photo do give a stark, but memorable image.

Nos 43013 and 43153 are the power for 1V60, the 13.43 Newcastle to Exeter, passing Elford on 3 May 2002. Ironically perhaps, No 43013 is now in yellow, being part of Network Rail's small fleet of power cars used to haul around the New Measurement Train. No 43153 has had an MTU power unit fitted and is in now in a deep blue livery, being part of First Great Western's fleet. *Adrian Kenny*

The Weymouth Quay line opened for goods in October 1865 and for passengers in August 1889 to serve the harbour and the Channel Island steamers. Apart from a break during World War 2, when the Channel Islands were occupied by German forces, the line continued to see goods traffic until 14 August 1972 and freight (oil) traffic until 16 September 1983. The last scheduled passenger trains over the branch were on 26 September 1987 after which the line remained open for the occasional charter or railtour.

On Sunday 2 May 1999, the first two trains since 1995 were run along the Weymouth Quay line in connection with Pathfinder Tours 'Wey-Farer' railtour. In this picture, No 73138 is seen hauling nine coaches down Commercial Road, with No 73106 out of sight on the rear, on the second of the two trips that day, the 1Z95 14.20 Yeovil Junction to Weymouth Quay. The 600hp diesel engines of the '73s' were not man enough to ascend the fearsome 1 in 50 of Upwey bank and so No 37250 was used to assist the tour between Weymouth Town and Yeovil Junction. *Adrian Kenny*

Porterbrook-liveried No 47817 rounds the curves at Westerleigh Junction, where the Midland Region joins the Western, with the 1V46 09.18 Manchester Piccadilly-Plymouth, on a beautiful 22 October 1997. Delivered from Crewe as D1611 in August 1964 it went initially to Landore depot. Staying in South Wales until September 1986 when, as No 47032, it went north to Gateshead, the locomotive was soon summoned to Crewe works for ETH fitting, emerging as No 47662. Long-range 3,238gal tanks were fitted in August 1989 and No 47817 was its next incarnation. By April 1996 it was owned by Porterbrook, and used as a spot hire locomotive. At this stage it and No 47807 were repainted into the then house colours of the leasing company, being released to traffic on April 25 1996. It soon ended up back in the Virgin ILRA pool and a repaint to Virgin red followed. A call to Brush at Loughborough came in July 2003 and its Sulzer 12LDA28 engine was removed and a General Motors 645-F3B-12 fitted; 57311 *Parker* is its current identity working for Virgin as a 'Thunderbird' locomotive. *Neil Higson*

Before the days of the internet, signalmen were pretty much the main source of information, a trip to Corby in the summer of 1997 being no exception. With the running of the train confirmed, a location in the Welland Valley was chosen to record the event.

Prior to negotiating the magnificent 82-arch Harringworth Viaduct, BSC blue-liveried No 60033 *Tees Steel Express* crawls past the photographer at Gretton, heading 6E40, the 10.23 Corby to Lackenby on 14 August.

Two Class 60s carried BSC's light blue colours, No 60006 *Scunthorpe Ironmaster* being the other example. The pair were unveiled during a ceremony at Scunthorpe in July 1997. British Steel was later taken over by Corus, resulting in both locomotives being reliveried in the Dutch company's silver scheme. *Paul Higgins*

**Opposite:** One of the more anticipated moves of 2002 was the reintroduction to mainline passenger duties of a 'Western' class diesel-hydraulic loco after a gap of a little less than 25 years. Withdrawn in 1976 after a working life of just 13 years, D1015 *Western Champion* was bought from BR by the Diesel Traction Group in 1980. There followed an extensive period of restoration, rebuilding the locomotive piece by piece, virtually from scratch. The locomotive returned to use on the Severn Valley Railway in 2000 to accumulate 1,000 (how ironic!) miles of running in order to satisfy the requirements to return it to mainline use.

On 23 February 2002, the dream became a reality when D1015 hauled the 'Western Pathfinder', a circular tour from Paddington to Paddington via Box, Bristol Temple Meads, Gloucester and Kemble.

With the exception of 2004, when the locomotive was undergoing transmission repairs, *Western Champion* has operated around half a dozen railtours each year. One of these was Pathfinder Tours' 'Western Quarryman' visiting Okehampton and Merehead. Here the locomotive trundles up the Meldon branch near Gunstone Mill with the 1Z46 05.39 Crewe to Okehampton on Saturday 15 March 2003, having taken over from No 46035 at Bristol Temple Meads. *Adrian Kenny*

One of the most amazing workings of 2001 occurred on 5 June. A very clean No 47810 *Porterbrook* failed at Didcot with an AWS fault, whilst working 1S54, the 05.50 Bournemouth to Glasgow Central. No 58020 *Doncaster Works* was hastily summoned from the stabling point. Running 45min late, the Mainline-branded '58' hauling the complete Virgin-liveried train heads towards Didcot North Junction. All was not well though, as the Ruston Paxman-engined freight machine partially failed at Banbury, where *Porterbrook* was revived, managing to push the 'Bone' to Coventry. The '58' then regained its health, completing the diesel-hauled part of the journey. *Mark Darby*

One of the most popular workings in the 1990s was the Liquid Petroleum Gas (LPG) flow from Furzebrook in Hampshire to Avonmouth in Bristol. No 47223 had the honour of hauling the inaugural train back in November 1990. Initially two trains a week would take the mixed load of butane and propane, but slowly, as production ramped up, the train frequency increased. By 1999 11 trains a week were not unknown, but then the slide started as production methods at the Wytch Farm facility changed, resulting in the gas being pumped back down the well. This, coupled with less oil being available, had the effect of reducing the frequency of trains until the final train ran on 22 July 2005. The wagons were soon on their way to Marcroft at Stoke and the majority were broken up with some haste as was the distribution depot at Avonmouth. Any gas production now goes out by road as required.

No 66120 hauls the penultimate 6V29 19.37 departure, seen near Worgret Junction, Wareham on 15 July 2005. Various types of traction had worked the services, with Classes 47, 58 and 60 being regular and the odd 33, 37 and 73 used in emergencies. *Neil Higson*

The Wylye Valley between Westbury and Salisbury does not normally see Freightliner Intermodal trains such as the one pictured here. However, when the Basingstoke to Reading line is shut for weekend engineering work, diversions are normally put in place through this picturesque part of the world.

Thus No 66503 *The Railway Magazine* finds itself on unfamiliar ground whilst hauling 4O14, the 04.32 SO Garston to Southampton past the delightfully-named Hanging Langford on Saturday 9 December 2006. *Adrian Kenny*

On the bright autumnal morning of 2 October 1996, Transrail-branded No 56066 approaches the embankment of the M1 motorway at Lockington Gates, with a Calverton colliery to Ironbridge power station merry-go-round (mgr) working. Lockington Gates is situated on the Sheet Stores Junction to Stenson Junction freight-only route. As for the locomotive, it was withdrawn in April 1999, and broken up at Hull's, Rotherham by mid-December 2005.

Back in 1996 the use of HAA hoppers was the typical mgr formation. Nowadays, Class 56 locomotives on coal trains are little more than a memory, as is the decline in use of HAA/HBA wagons, with EWS, Freightliner and GBRF all preferring high-capacity bogie wagons. *Paul Higgins*

No 73107 *Spitfire* pulls away from Barnham Junction, past the splendid semaphore signals, on its way to Bognor Regis with the 1Z74 16.18 Littlehampton-London Bridge 'Blueberry Fool' railtour on 1 April 2006. The tour had arrived at Littlehampton from Cannon Street via Hastings, Eastbourne, Newhaven Marine and Brighton!

Still in 'Dutch' livery, which it had received during its BR days, when it was named

*Redhill 1844-1994*, No 73107 was withdrawn by EWS in 2002 as surplus to requirements. After overhaul by Fragonset at Derby, it was soon re-registered and back out on the main line as a hire locomotive, by then painted in Fragonset's freight black colour scheme. Due to the collapse of FM Rail, No 73107 was sold onto RT Rail Tours, which thankfully still operates the locomotive on the main line, but now in its grey colour scheme. *Neil Higson*

To the welcome surprise of the cameramen gathered at Great Brington, to record diverted West Coast expresses on the beautifully clear autumn afternoon of Sunday 18 October 1998, unique EWS-liveried No 31466 appeared from around the corner, working 6P35, a 13.00 Bletchley to Rugby train of spent ballast. The joy was compounded as the working was only a few minutes behind 'Mainline' blue liveried No 37248, also on engineers' duties. No 31466, the former 31115/D5536 was the sole class recipient of EWS colours, specially painted at Bescot depot for Toton's 1998 open weekend. At the time of writing (Summer 2007) No 31466 had just entered the world of preservation on the Dean Forest Railway, after a lengthy period of storage at Old Oak Common depot. *Mark Darby*

On occasions when engineering works closes the Severn Tunnel for maintenance, First Great Western (FGW) Paddington to South Wales trains are diverted down the Golden Valley through Kemble and thence via Gloucester and Chepstow to pick up their original route at Severn Tunnel Junction.

This is why an unidentified Class 180 Adelante unit can be seen coasting alongside the River Severn on the approach to Lydney. The working is the 17.07 London Paddington to Swansea and the date is Sunday 26 June 2005.

The 14 Adelantes were built by Alstom and, after testing, introduced by FGW in 2001 to meet its franchise commitment to provide half hourly services to Cardiff. In later years, the units were mostly employed on trains along the Cotswold line to Worcester and Hereford, where their acceleration, 125mph capability and superior comfort to Turbo type units made them ideally suited. Despite being thought of as internally superior to Voyagers, they proved troublesome to operate and maintain and upon completion of the HST refurbishment programme, FGW took them off lease. *Adrian Kenny*

Whether it be a RES Class 86, or one of the Railfreight Distribution Class 90s decorated in one of the 'European' liveries, the long-distance 1S96 almost always produced decent motive power.

On 23 April 2001, Belgian SNCB blue and yellow liveried No 90028 *Vrachtverbinding* storms away from Stowe Hill Tunnel, near Weedon, with a rake of RES liveried vans forming 1S96, the 16.00 London to Glasgow Shieldmuir. The Belgian colours were applied in 1992.

When first introduced in 1987, the class suffered with a few teething problems, settling down however to reliably cover many thousands of miles. *Paul Higgins*

Crown Point allocated No 86238 *European Community*, supporting the exceptionally fine turquoise Anglia livery, motors through lush Suffolk countryside, close to the boundary with Essex, at Brantham with an almost complete rake of Mk 2 vehicles, interrupted only by the inclusion of a Mk 3 buffet, forming the day's 15.40 Norwich-London Liverpool Street on 12 June 2000. The EEC or European Economic Community was founded on 25 March 1957 by the signing of the Treaty of Rome. The word 'Economic' was dropped in 1992 after the Maastricht Treaty. The electrification of the former Great Eastern main line continued to be energised in sections as it was extended from Colchester. Class 86s commenced operation through to Ipswich Town on 13 May 1985, a locomotive change being required for the run into Norfolk until electricity brought Norwich out of the dark ages in May 1987. No 86238 started life as E3116. *Mark Darby*

No 37417 *Highland Region,*
formerly D6969 and 37269,
races past Point of Ayr Colliery,
near Prestatyn on the North Wales
coast on 3 August 1996, with a
Crewe-Bangor service, hauling five
Regional Railways liveried Mk 1s
and a Rivera-owned chocolate and
cream Mk 1 at the rear, added to
strengthen the set. Just 20 days
later the mine was finally shut,
after 106 years of production.
In its heyday in 1953, 738 men
were employed but this slowly
dwindled as coal faces were closed
culminating in total closure and
demolition. The pit's own colliery
wharf was used for many years
to ship the coal, but rail was the
preferred option in later years, most
of the production being taken to the
local coal yards and power stations
such as the nearby Fiddlers Ferry.
*Neil Higson*

Each night for the past 10 years or more, the only automotive train to operate in Wales has been a service from Dagenham to Bridgend and Swansea. One train would operate, dropping off the majority of its Ford vans and Cargowaggons at Bridgend, and then continuing with its remaining IVAs to Swansea Burrows.

Thus, on a pleasantly sunny Tuesday 25 May 2004, No 09101 finds itself trundling down the short branch from Swansea Burrows sidings to the Visteon plant with the four IVAs of automotive parts that No 66228 had dropped off just a few hours earlier. Behind the train can be glimpsed the Gower Chemicals plant which uses the former Danygraig steam shed.

Rail traffic to the Visteon plant finished just a few months after this photograph was taken and today the branch, along with half of Burrows sidings and many of the nearby dock lines, has been lifted, a far cry from the days in 2000 and 2001 when two pilot engines were required at Swansea Burrows Yard for the various coal, steel, container and automotive services emanating from the area. *Adrian Kenny*

One of the highlights of the heritage traction calendar over the last few years have been the FA Cup Final specials to Cardiff. Invariably, at least one team came from either Liverpool or Manchester, which brought interesting locomotive-hauled trains down the Marches.

On Saturday 22 May 2002, whilst *en route* to the annual South Wales pilgrimage, a short detour off the M5 near Michaelwood services produced a bonus, in the shape of No 40145, which was duly photographed making for Devon. Tipping the scales at a whopping 133 tonnes

(only the production 'Peaks' were heavier), the former D345 whistles its way through Damery with a complementary rake of Mk 2s forming 1Z40, the 07.00 Crewe to Plymouth 'Western Whistler II' railtour.

As a brief footnote, for any 'footie' fans the 2002 FA Cup final boasted an incredibly rare appearance by South London's finest. Inevitably though, Millwall succumbed to a 0-3 defeat by Manchester United. *Paul Higgins*

Low winter sun illuminates Railfreight Distribution-branded No 90022 *Freightconnection* powering along the West Coast mainline at Heamies Farm, Norton Bridge, whilst hauling 4A01, the 10.48 Trafford Park to Wembley Intermodal service on 20 November 1999. Freightconnection was organised by the Railfreight Distribution sector of British Rail in 1992, to promote an increase in freight traffic between France, Germany, Belgium and the UK upon the opening of the Channel Tunnel. No 90022 was named at this event along with three other Class 90s, No 90130 *Fretconnection* in 'Sybic' class specific orange and grey (this is not the standard SNCF livery), 90129 *Frachtverbindungen* in DB red livery and No 90128 *Vrachtverbinding* outshopped in the smart house colours of SNCB, the Belgian state railway. *Mark Darby*

Royal-liveried No 47799 *Prince Henry* has led a busy life since it was released into traffic on 23 July 1965 as D1654. In the next 39 years it was numbered 47070, 47620 and 47835 and finally withdrawn from the active EWS fleet as No 47799 in February 2004. It is currently in long-term storage at Ferrybridge.

One of two Royal 47's dedicated in 1995, it was often used on prestigious charters such as the VSOE. On just such a duty, 1Z91 the 13.55 Exeter St David's-Plymouth, it can be seen heading past the River Teign near Bishopsteignton on 29 April 2000. The Mk 3 sleeper behind the locomotive is for the staff accommodation, when working away from the normal base at London Victoria. A blue generator van breaks up the livery of the beautiful 1920s-30s Orient Express coaches which can be seen mainly in the South of England all year, allowing people to sample luxurious rail travel from a bygone era. *Neil Higson*

**Opposite:** Under threatening skies, No 43151 is on the rear of the 1C11 07.33 Paddington-Penzance passing the old pumping station at Crofton on the Berks & Hants line, or 'mule', or 'desert' as it is variously known. The date was Saturday 28 September 2002 and this was the last booked day of First Great Western (FGW)-operated locomotive-hauled daytime passenger trains.

These locomotive-hauled trains had been introduced only as stopgap measure until FGW's problematical fleet of Adelantes could be fully deployed from the start of the new timetable the next day. From that point on, only the sleepers would be booked for locomotive haulage with Adelantes and HSTs covering everything else. *Adrian Kenny*

Until 1965, when the passenger service was withdrawn, the beautiful Fowey Valley echoed to the relaxed tones of ex-Great Western 0-4-2 Class 14XX tanks shuttling back and forth between Lostwithiel and Fowey with a solitary autocoach. The branch is now freight-only, the exclusive preserve of china clay traffic.

On 9 July 1997 Transrail's aptly named No 37674 *St Blaise Church 1445-1995* returns an empty rake of CDA hoppers past an attractive selection of multicoloured boats as it passes over the causeway at Golant, heading back from Fowey to Burngullow.

Beginning life as D6869, the locomotive became 37169 under the TOPS renumbering. The name commemorates the 550th anniversary of the church, which is just outside St Blazey. The naming ceremony occurred at St Blazey depot on 12 December 1995 and was performed by the then vicar's nine-year-old son. *Paul Higgins*

Although not as spectacular as some of the Scottish and Cumbrian vantage points on offer, the Peak district around Buxton boasts some pretty good photographic gems, not to mention respite, when the Moorland elements take a change for the worse, in 'Bill's Fish & Chips' – possibly one of the finest chippies in the land! On a bitterly cold 9 November 2007, Freightliner's No 66527

*Don Raider* presents a fine sight as it slowly negotiates the remains of the Buxton to Ashbourne route, at Brierlow Bar, with 6M44, the 05.43 Cottam power station to Dowlow empty hoppers. The power station at Cottam lies at the end of the now truncated branch that once ran from Clarborough Junction to Saxilby. *Mark Darby*

No 50017 in LMS 'Coronation Scot' livery runs through the Avon Valley, near Bath, on a hot 22 July 2000. The privately-owned engine was taking an ECS working (5Z27 16.37 Westbury-Bath Spa) back to Bath after servicing, ultimately working to Manchester Victoria. Its train, the VSOE-run 'Northern Belle' was introduced on 31 May 2000 as a sister to the traditional London Victoria-based train. Initially privately-owned locomotives were used, Nos 50017, 55019 and 55009 being the regular engines, crewed mainly by a team of Crewe-based drivers.

This 10-year contract with the locomotive owners came to a sudden end on 8 October 2000 when it was announced that EWS would crew and supply power for the train.

No 50017 was formerly named *Royal Oak* after the famous World War I 'Dreadnought' class battleship and was the 41st Class 50 to be withdrawn, on 9 September 1991 with a main generator fault. It was soon purchased for preservation, and is currently being repaired by the Birmingham Railway Museum, Tyseley. *Neil Higson*

On the 18 April 2007 'Thunderbird' No 57308 *Tin Tin* glides through the spectacular Cumbrian Fells in the Lune Gorge, with the Amec-Spie operated 6Z57, the 13.29 Carlisle Yard to Chirk, with timber bound for the Kronospan works. The train is formed of KFAs, which had recently been converted from former GE Rail Services vans at WH Davis, Shirebrook. The first run of these wagons was earlier in the month, on the 5th. No 57308 had carried four previous numbers during its career: D1677, 47091, 47647 and 47846. Much of the locomotive's career has been spent allocated to the Western Region named *Thor*, who rather aptly is the Norse god of thunder. The 'Thunderbird' concept was officially launched at London Euston, at a ceremony on 17 June 2002, where No 57301 was unveiled by the creator of the 'Thunderbirds' television series, Gerry Anderson, and various Virgin Trains officials. *Mark Darby*

No 60008 is captured in silhouette whilst crossing Eckington Viaduct on Thursday 17 November 2005. Its 11 JNA/JXA and MBA wagons are loaded with scrap to feed the hungry electric arc furnaces at Celsa Steel (UK)'s works in Cardiff, running as 6V97, the 13.39 TThO from Beeston.

Freightliner Heavy Haul (FHH) won the Beeston contract from EWS in April 2006 and the southbound train could then be seen routed south via the North & West route through Hereford, as well as the line through Cheltenham, depending on the requirements of the day. The last FHH-operated train ran on Monday 16 July 2007 and EWS took over again from the end of the same month. *Adrian Kenny*